FUCK THE TORIES

SPHERE

First published in Great Britain in 2023 by Sphere

10 9 8 7 6 5 4 3 2 1

Hardback ISBN 9781408730997

Designed by Studio Polka
Printed and bound in Great Britain by Clays Ltd, Elcograf S.p.A.
Papers used by Sphere are from well-managed forests and other responsible sources.

Sphere
An imprint of
Little, Brown Book Group
Carmelite House
50 Victoria Embankment
London EC4Y 0DZ

An Hachette UK Company
www.hachette.co.uk
www.littlebrown.co.uk

For the #FuckTheTories crew. Society is in ruins, the planet is on fire, and most of us will never own a house, but at least you've got a good book to leave on the coffee table next time your parents pop round to moan about immigrants.

FUCK THE TORIES: AN ACTIVITY BOOK

Some people* in the United Kingdom of Great Britain and Northern Ireland are inclined to say the following:

Fuck austerity. Fuck cronyism. Fuck bedroom tax. Fuck not preventing sewage in the sea. Fuck raising tuition fees. Fuck breaking your own Covid rules. Fuck luxury sheds. Fuck 'Dancing Queen'. Fuck non-existent hospitals. Fuck cuts to mental health funding. Fuck wrecking the economy. Fuck NHS privatisation. Fuck driving to a castle for an eye test. Fuck writing lies on the side of a bus. Fuck sending immigrants to Rwanda. Fuck handing contracts to mates. Fuck threatening to privatise Channel 4. Fuck luxury flat renovations. Fuck partying during lockdown. Fuck deporting the Windrush generation. Fuck proroguing Parliament. Fuck U-turns. Fuck cuts to nurses' bursaries. Fuck fox hunting. Fuck misleading the Queen. Fuck demonising unions. Fuck cuts to public services. Fuck unkept promises.

But most of all...

...FUCK THE TORIES.

Are they right? In this book you'll find puzzles, activities, quizzes and much more that have been inspired by Tory rule since 2010, plus some historic Tory times. We hope by the end of it you'll have worked out whether the above statement represents your thoughts or not. Be sure to let us know on social media with #fuckthetories.

—

*Obviously we are of the #fuckthetories crew and therefore do believe in this statement. No, we don't feel the need to hold up the failings of the other political parties. This is because, at the time of writing, the Tories have been in power for more than a decade and so we feel entitled to hold them to account for the current state of the UK. If you would like a 'Fuck Labour' or 'Fuck the Lib Dems' or 'Fuck the SNP' book do go ahead and write your own.

And yes, we are sure you can argue that the Tories have done some good things – some people might even think the things we've discussed in this book are good things. If you want that sort of account please see the *Daily Mail*. This is a book about the things the Tories have done that we deem to be bad or embarrassing. If there wasn't enough material, we wouldn't have been able to write this book. We hope you enjoy it, and that maybe we'll even be able to change a right-wing mind or two.

AWFUL TORY VOTING RECORDS

Being elected as an MP is the ultimate privilege; a chance to represent your constituents and vote for ideas that will improve society, but, in our opinion, it doesn't appear that the Conservative Party got the memo. Here are ten statements about Tory voting records, but in each instance the subject has been removed. Can you complete them using the list on the opposite page?[1]

1. Between 2013 – 2019, MP for North East Somerset Jacob Rees-Mogg voted against .... nine times.

2. Between 2001 – 2010, MP for Maidenhead Theresa May voted against .... forty-nine times.

3. Between 2002 – 2004, MP for Christchurch Christopher Chope voted against .... six times.

4. Between 2012 – 2013, MP for Stone Bill Cash voted against .... five times.

5. Between 2012 – 2015, MP for Lichfield Michael Fabricant voted against .... twelve times.

6. Between 2008 – 2022, MP for Raleigh and Wickford Mark Francois voted against .... one hundred and thirteen times.

7. Between 2010 – 2015, MP for Suffolk Coastal Thérèse Coffey voted against .... four times.

8. Between 2011 – 2015, MP for Chingford and Woodford Green Iain Duncan Smith voted against .... fourteen times.

9. Between 2013 – 2014, MP for South Northamptonshire Andrea Leadsom voted against .... four times.

10. Between 2015 – 2022, MP for Uxbridge and South Ruislip Boris Johnson voted against .... eight times.

A. The hunting ban

B. More EU integration

C. Increasing the tax rate applied to income over £150,000

D. Slowing the rise in rail fares

E. Equal gay rights

F. Bankers' bonus tax

G. Greater regulation of gambling

H. Labour's anti-terrorism laws

I. Higher taxes on banks

J. Smoking bans

MATCH THE QUOTE TO THE TORY

Below are ten disturbing quotes. Can you match each one up
with the relevant Tory MP named on the opposite page?

1. I would go further and say that it is absolutely ridiculous that people should choose to go around looking like letter boxes.

2. [After being photographed wearing blackface] Are you saying a black man can't get into a fancy dress party as a white man? That we must stay in our racial silos?

3. The problem that we have with illegal migration, and we should be very clear about this, is that the majority of people are not fleeing persecution, they are asylum shopping and that is why they should be claiming asylum in other countries.

4. Feminists are now amongst the most obnoxious bigots.

5. [Responding to reports that a Tory MP was being investigated for sexual assault] I am expecting a strong turnout of Conservative MPs at Prime Minister's Questions today. Not only to demonstrate their strong support for #Boris (!!). BUT also to prove they are NOT the one told by the Chief Whip to stay at home. I'll be there!☻

6. The definition of marriage and the definition of sex is for ordinary and complete sex to have taken place. Same-sex couples cannot meet this requirement.

7. [On the Grenfell Tower tragedy] I think if either of us were in a fire, whatever the fire brigade said, we would leave the burning building.

8. Katy works for me. She is single & earns less than 30k, rents a room for £775pcm in Central London, has student debt, £120 a month on travelling to work saves money every month, goes on foreign holidays & does not need to use a foodbank. Katy makes my point really well.

8. (On the Commons dining area) The service was absolutely fantastic because there was three-to-one service – three servants for each person sitting down.

10. The British people deserve to know which party is serious about stopping the invasion of our southern coast – and which party is not.

Suella Braverman

Jacob Rees-Mogg

Christopher Chope

Michael Fabricant

Nadine Dorries

Priti Patel

Lee Anderson

Dominic Raab

Boris Johnson

Desmond Swayne

TORIES BY NUMBERS: PANDEMIC EDITION

Although Boris Johnson's lockdown antics have hogged headlines with regards the Covid-19 pandemic, the Tory government's handling of the crisis resulted in the UK having the sixth highest death toll in the world[2] – for context, we have the twenty-first largest population. The following numbers all relate to the pandemic. Can you match them up with what they represent?

~~~~~~

1. 37,000,000,000

2. 50

3. 5

4. 100,000

5. 4,000,000,000

6. 47

7. 2

8. 4,500,000,000

9. 300,034,974,000

10. 39.1

A. Number of Cobra meetings about the developing Covid outbreak that Boris Johnson skipped, according to Michael Gove.

B. Amount (in pounds) lost to Covid fraud that a government taskforce was set up to chase before being shut down in January 2023 by HMRC, which claimed that pursuing the money didn't provide the best value for the taxpayer.

C. Distance (in metres) that people from different households were required to maintain in order to comply with the government's social distancing rules.

D. The number of daily Covid tests that health secretary Matt Hancock was trying to hit by the end of April 2020 (It later emerged that he was concerned prioritising tests in care homes would hamper his efforts to hit his target).

E. The percentage the government subsidised for food and non-alcoholic drinks during Rishi Sunak's Eat Out to Help Out scheme. (A study by University of Warwick economist Thiemo Fetzer has claimed the scheme increased Covid infections between eight and seventeen percent.)

F. The two-year budget (in pounds) set by the government in 2020 for the NHS Test and Trace app.

G. The value (in pounds) of PPE purchased by the government during the first year of the pandemic which was later burned after being found to be unusable.

H. The number of companies that were awarded lucrative PPE contracts after referrals from government officials, in what became known as the 'VIP lane'.

I. The percentage of A-level results that were downgraded in 2020 as a result of the algorithm spearheaded by then-education secretary Gavin Williamson.

J. The number that then Home Secretary Priti Patel used during a press conference on 11 April 2020, when talking about how many Covid tests had been carried out in the UK to that point.

FREE SCHOOL MEALS WORDSEARCH

In October 2020, a total of three hundred and twenty Conservative MPs voted against free school meals for hungry children over the holidays[3], despite a month's-long battle with interim leader of the opposition Marcus Rashford. Although it doesn't quite have the same nutritional value, the below wordsearch contains all the ingredients for a classic school lunch. How many can you find?

```
L O T V H P Y M G Z I I M G D E Q A N P X P M
R Q L U M P Y M A S H E D P O T A T O E N W L
A P L X A R D X K K W B S B U T C W K M P U S
U D R S Z H V X E J F V X D T O W F C Z G U P
I U P M Z B I R F G U E L I Y S Q C N I G D O
O S I H I Y F G F Q G W S R T Z P P Q U L A O
R E N P P V V X A F Y L O P Y L O R M A J I H
Z I K J E Y S D A H I Q P E Q B D R J H K E I
L P C W R W E Z J E I D R A Z R K F A U V Z T
O E U A A C F J G M J P S P F S C L S U U C T
T S S R U W N G I O H H A H S N U Y T R N O E
D E T V Q A L R J N W O K G I G Q X J G L O H
R E A F S B A S T R A T E K A L F N R O C V G
S H R I N Z G A O H C R U C B K J E W N I B A
V C D Y C A U L I F L O W E R C H E E S E Z P
P T J H G F E U I O F Q B G H P Z M L G O U S
```

Pink custard

Square pizza

Cornflake tart

Lumpy mashed potato

Cauliflower cheese

Jam roly-poly

Cheese pie

Spaghetti hoops

Sponge pudding

FINISH THE LIMERICK

Here are some limericks about Tory MPs, but each has a word
missing. Feel free to fill in the blanks with anything that rhymes!

~~~~~~

There once was a man called Matt,
Who was largely considered a .... ,
He had a good job, but thought with his nob,
And that was the end of that.

There was an old lady called Priti,
Whose policies were evil and .... ,
With a smirk and a sneer, she'd often appear,
In front of the Select Committee.

There was an MP called Dom,
Who thought you could drive to the Somme,
His staff found him blunt, a bit of a .... ,
So he bullied them 'til he was gone.

TORY PUB QUIZ: ROUND ONE

What could be more fun than a pub quiz all about the Tories? Connecting a car battery to your genitals? Wading through an open sewer? Going to a Right Said Fred concert? Well if you can't be bothered to do any of those things, have a go at these ten questions instead.

1. In August 2018, Theresa May was mocked for dancing awkwardly with schoolchildren during a visit to which country?

A: Tunisia
B: South Africa
C: Mozambique
D: Kenya

2. In December 2022, which MP revealed that they don't know what bishops do for a living after accusing them of 'using the pulpit to preach from' regarding the government's Rwanda deportation scheme?

A: Penny Mordaunt
B: Nadine Dorries
C: Jonathan Gullis
D: Suella Braverman

3. In a chilling sign of incompetence to come, what did Liz Truss manage to do after launching her leadership bid in July 2022?

A: Get her head stuck in a recycling bin
B: Slip on a banana skin
C: Get lost trying to exit the room
D: Walk into a disabled toilet

4. In 2012 the Tories launched the 'Bedroom Tax', which reduced housing benefits for those living in a council house with an unoccupied bedroom. What was its official title?

A: Unoccupied Space Act
B: Excess Housing Penalty
C: Housing Suitability Act
D: Under-occupancy penalty

5. In 2023 it emerged that Suella Braverman had committed which driving offence?

A: Speeding
B: Being uninsured
C: Not wearing a seatbelt
D: Texting at the wheel

6. Which Tory MP and former minister appeared on *I'm a Celebrity ... Get Me Out Of Here!* in 2012, eating an ostrich's anus and a camel's toe in the process?

A: Jeremy Hunt
B: Iain Duncan Smith
C: Nadine Dorries
D: Amber Rudd

7. The Euro 2020 final between England and Italy was watched by thirty-one million people in the UK, but Lee Anderson was not one of them. Why did he miss the game?

A: He was involved in a minor car accident
B: He had a power cut
C: He boycotted it due to players taking the knee
D: He accidentally locked himself in his garage

8. In 2021, which government minister flew to thirty different countries in six months, despite their status as president of the Cop26 climate summit?

A: Steve Baker
B: Esther McVey
C: Kwasi Kwarteng
D: Alok Sharma

9. What job title was given to Jacob Rees-Mogg by Boris Johnson in February 2022?

A: Minister for Parliamentary Standards and Government Integrity
B: Minister for Brexit Opportunities and Government Efficiency
C: Minister for Post-Brexit Trade and Global Opportunities
D: Minister for Falling Asleep in the House of Commons

10. In August 2021, which MP was spotted dancing (or at least, something resembling dancing) at a nightclub in Aberdeen?

A: Sajid Javid
B: Michael Gove
C: Mark Francois
D: Steve Baker

BARNARD CASTLE EYE TEST

In 2020 Dominic Cummings changed the world of optometry forever by driving from Durham to Barnard Castle to test his eyesight. Can you retrace his (not topographically-accurate) journey by navigating the maze below?* (*For the most authentic experience, squint your eyes until the maze appears blurry)

NET ZERO (FUCKS GIVEN)

We're not sure the Tory government cares all that much about climate change and the environment, and we'll tell you for why. From the coalition government's decision to scrap energy efficiency funding[4], to Boris Johnson scrapping the Green Homes Grant[5], to Liz Truss trying (and ultimately failing, due to her short time in No 10) to bring back fracking[6], to Rishi Sunak's record for using private jets and helicopters[7], we don't have a great deal of confidence right now that the UK will be anywhere close to net zero by 2050. Are you more environmentally conscious than a Tory? Below are ten everyday activities, but can you arrange them (lowest to highest) in terms of their carbon footprint?[8]

Taking a hot shower for 10 minutes

Going for a 30 minute walk

Flying from London to New York in a commercial jet

Boiling a kettle

Making one Google search

Using a mobile phone for one hour

Eating one banana

Drinking a pint of beer

Using an eco-friendly lightbulb (18W) for 4 hours

Eating one tomato

REAL OR FAKE TORY EXPENSES CLAIM?

Below are ten statements about Tory expense claims, but can you work out which are genuine, and which ones are made up?

1. Iain Duncan Smith claimed £39 for a single breakfast (despite previously claiming that he could comfortably live on just £53 a week).

2. Paul Beresford claimed two iPod Shuffles in the space of a week after leaving one on a train.

3. David Heathcote-Amory claimed £380 worth of horse manure.

4. Former Tory MP Peter Viggers claimed over £30,000 in gardening expenses, including a 'floating duck island' worth £1,645.

5. Michelle Donelan claimed fifteen scratch cards on expenses after including them in her lunchtime meal deals, but paid the money back after winning £1,000.

6. Andrew Selous claimed 55p for a mug of Horlicks.

7. Chris Heaton-Harris claimed a variety of magazine subscriptions, including Total Guitar, Classic Rock, and The Beano.

8. Tory Peer Ed Vaizey claimed 8p for a 350-yard car journey.

9. James Arbuthnot attempted to claim £43.56 for three garlic peelers.

10. Pauline Latham claimed £204 for four tickets to Mamma Mia! In London's West End.

HATE CRIME NATION

In November 2022 the House of Commons Library published an in-depth report on hate crime statistics in the UK[9]. It found that between 2013 and 2022 the number of police-recorded hate crimes had more than tripled in England and Wales. Some argue this is because the Tory government demonises minority groups – but whether you believe that or not, why isn't more being done to tackle these numbers? See if you can answer these five questions about the findings of the report.

~~~~~~

I. In 2012 there were 313 recorded hate crimes against transgender people in England and Wales. How many were recorded in 2022?

A: 1,032
B: 2,567
C: 3,879
D: 4,355

2. Which police force area was found to have the highest number of total hate crimes per 100,000 population, with 457 recorded in 2021/2022 alone?

A: Metropolitan Police
B: West Midlands
C: Greater Manchester
D: Leicestershire

3. Between 2010 and 2022, by what percentage did recorded hate crimes on people with disabilities increase in Scotland?

A: 512 per cent
B: 860 per cent
C: 1,287 per cent
D: 1,428 per cent

4. Between 2016 and 2017, the number of recorded hate crimes in England and Wales leapt from 49,419 to 62,685 with which motivating factor?

A: Race
B: Religion
C: Sexual orientation
D: Disability

5. During the Covid-19 pandemic, there was a 15 per cent increase in attacks on what?

A: Asian-owned businesses
B: Mosques
C: Synagogues
D: Non-white medical staff

TORY MATHS

You probably know by now that Rishi Sunak <3 maths (in fairness we expect having a good grasp of the subject makes it much easier to count the gold tiles in your swimming pool) – outlining in 2023 a plan to make kids learn the subject up until the age of 18. In that vein, here are five maths problems to solve.

1. A minister's friend receives a lucrative contract to provide one million pieces of PPE (specifically, high-end bin bags). If only twelve percent of the order is fulfilled, how many pieces of PPE will be provided?

2. If Boris is walking East, then performs a one hundred and eighty-degree U-turn, followed by seven more U-turns, and then one final U-turn for good measure, in which direction is he now travelling?

3. Chris gives a shipping contract to a company with zero ferries in its northern fleet, zero ferries in its Atlantic fleet, and zero ferries in its southern fleet. How many ferries are there in total?

4. Matt and Gina are standing two meters apart. If Matt moves ninety-seven centimetres closer to Gina, and Gina moves ninety-eight centimetres closer to Matt, how far apart are they now standing?

5. Three million people use a food bank in January. If that number increases by twenty-three percent in February, how many people are now using a food bank?

THE TORY PROPERTY LADDER

First time buyer in Tory Britain? Here's your very own property ladder! Rungs not available at time of publication so you'll have to draw them on yourself.

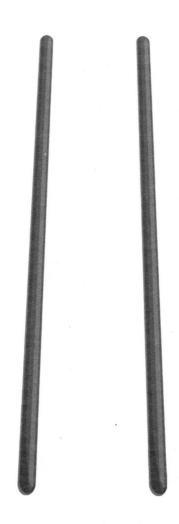

TORIES:
A HISTORY

Finding it hard to respect Tories isn't a new concept. The answers to the following crossword all relate to shady stuff the Tories got up to before the turn of the century.

DOWN

1. The informal name given to the 1992 sterling crisis, which had such an impact on the British economy that John Major drafted a resignation letter.

2. '............ Heath' – the nickname given to Ted Heath by Private Eye following his abolition of resale price maintenance in 1964.

4. 'New Labour, new ....' – the infamous Tory attack poster portraying Tony Blair with demonic eyes in the lead up to the 1997 general election.

5. 'Cash for ....' – the 1994 sleaze scandal that involved Tory MPs Neil Hamilton and Tim Smith, as well as Harrods owner Mohamed Al-Fayed

7. .... affair – the name given to the bitter dispute between Margaret Thatcher and defence secretary Michael Heseltine (who would end up resigning over the matter) regarding the future of a British helicopter company.

ACROSS

3. The contaminated .... scandal – a crisis that took place during the premiership of Margaret Thatcher which the Guardian described as 'the worst treatment disaster in the history of the NHS'.[10]

6. The MP who was especially popular with John Major and famously issued a warning about the risk of salmonella in British eggs. Was also instrumental in Jimmy Savile gaining unprecedented access to Broadmoor psychiatric hospital.[11]

8. Arthur .... – trade unionist who went up against Margaret Thatcher's government by leading the 1984–85 UK miners' strike.

9. Complete the following phrase, which was coined in 1970 when then education secretary Margaret Thatcher ended the provision of free school milk: 'Thatcher, Thatcher, milk ....'[12]

QUICKFIRE BREXIT ROUND

Let's be honest, nobody wants to relive the Brexit years, so the aim of this round is to get through it as quickly as possible. Here are ten questions about the Tories' complete and utter incompetence in dealing with the UK's exit from the European Union. If you can answer all these questions in 60 seconds give yourself an extra ten points.

I. What did David Davis, Dominic Raab, and Steve Barclay have in common?

2. The day after the EU referendum David Cameron resigned. What peculiar thing did he do as he turned from the lectern and walked back inside No 10?

3. Following Theresa May's snap election in April 2017, which she called in the hope it would increase her majority (it did not), which party did she have to form a dubious alliance with?

4. A proposed protocol to prevent an evident border in Ireland, which – despite months of development from the UK and the EU – never actually came into force, was called the Irish what? It begins with B.

5. On 20 March 2019, Theresa May wrote to the President of the European Council to embarrassingly request the first of three extensions to which Article?

6. In the period leading up to the EU referendum Michael Gove, Steve Baker, Priti Patel, Anne-Marie Trevelyan, and Douglas Carswell were all members of a hardline parliamentary group which solely focuses on the UK's relationship with the EU. What is it called?

7. Prominent Leave campaigners including Boris Johnson and Penny Mordaunt were accused of making misleading and false claims about which country – with a then population of 81 million – joining the EU?

8. During an interview with The Sun on 3 November 2019, how did Boris Johnson describe his proposed Brexit deal?[13]

9. In June 2018, a company called Somerset Capital set up a hedge fund in (EU member nation) Ireland, despite one of its co-founders being a staunch Leave supporter. Who was it?

10. In July 2020, Parliament's Intelligence and Security Committee published a report which accused the UK government of avoiding investigating whether which country interfered with public opinion?[14]

NOTHING SAYS TORY BRITAIN LIKE ... HOMELESS CHILDREN?

In January 2023, research by Shelter showed that at least 271,000 people were recorded as homeless in England, including 123,000 children[15] – despite the Tories pledge to end the homelessness crisis by 2024 in their 2019 general election manifesto[16]. Can you place the following towns and cities in order of the number of children that are homeless and living in temporary accommodation? 1 = highest, 10 = lowest.

~~~~~~

Basildon

Birmingham

Brighton and Hove

Harlow

Hastings

London

Luton

Manchester

Milton Keynes

Slough

LEAVING A TOWN NEAR YOU

Research published in 2019 showed councils had sold off £9.1 billion worth of assets between 2015-2018 alone. This was done to cover budget holes, which included redundancy payments (redundancies were necessary because of central government cuts). Assets sold included playing fields, libraries, youth clubs, parks and community centres.[17] Imagine the below as a made up town. Using the clues, can you figure out which shape is which 'asset'?

Assets
library, youth club, park, playing field, community centre

THE TOWN

Clues:

Neither the playing field nor the community centre are opposite the library.

The library is next to the youth club on the same row.

The youth club has an asset to the left and right of it.

The playing field is next to the community centre on the same row.

The park isn't diagonally situated from the community centre.

JOIN THE DOTS

A certain Tory MP is on their way to work. Join the dots to find out who it is!

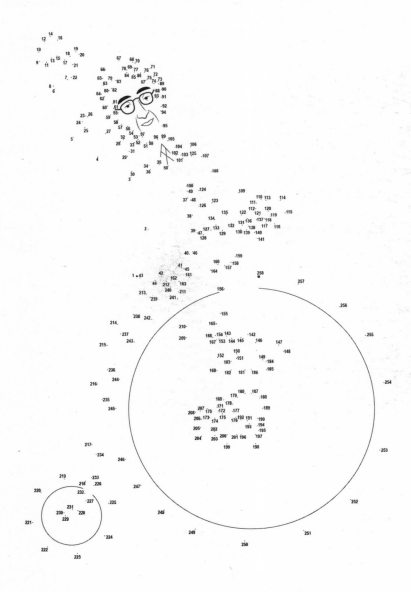

DECORATE YOUR OWN
LUXURY WALLPAPER

One of the perks of living in 10 Downing Street is that you can decorate it however you like, no matter the cost (because someone else is footing the bill, naturally). Here is a blank wall for you to put your very own stamp on.

#TORYSCMU –
ANAGRAMS ROUND ONE

The following words, people, and phrases are more muddled
up than a Liz Truss interview answer. Can you unscramble
the Tory anagrams using the clues provided?

~~~~~~

1. **ARROGANT TALLEST** (two words). Former Downing Street press secretary who was thrown under the bus at the start of the partygate saga after footage emerged of her joking about drinks at No 10 during lockdown.

2. **ERECT** (one word). Popular holiday destination where Dominic Raab was accused of paddleboarding while Kabul fell, leading to his infamous 'the sea was closed that day' defence.

3. **OCEANIC** (one word). Class-A drug that Michael Gove admitted taking in an interview with the Daily Mail during the Conservative Party leadership contest in 2019.[18]

4. **RIP STUN** (one word). Root vegetable championed by Thérèse Coffey at the height of the UK fruit and veg shortages in early 2023.

5. **BENDY LEVEE VEG** (two words). Russian/British 'businessman' appointed to the House of Lords by Boris Johnson in 2020, despite security concerns relating to his father, a former KGB agent.[19]

6. **GNATHARM** (one word). Town in Lincolnshire that became the UK's number one tourist hotspot for pigeons when a statue of Margaret Thatcher was unveiled there in 2022.

7. **LISPS UNDULANT** (two words). A phrase used by Winston Churchill in his famous 'This was their finest hour' speech in 1940. Has in recent years been adapted by numerous Tories to describe the supposed golden future of post-Brexit Britain.

8. **RAD ROACH SMURFS** (two words). English footballer who has challenged the Tories on several occasions regarding free school dinners, often more effectively than the opposition.

9. **APACHE FED SCANS** (three words). Slogan used by the government at the height of the Covid pandemic (which they were later found to have not taken particularly seriously themselves).

10. **FANCIER INJURER** (two words). American technology entrepreneur who allegedly provided one-on-one IT lessons for Boris Johnson while he was the mayor of London.[20]

HOW MUCH????

One of the Tories' biggest failures is arguably their disregard for the UK's spiralling housing crisis. As of February 2020, there were around 800,000 fewer home-owning households aged under-45 than when the Tories came to power in 2010[21], and in November 2019 the National Audit Office claimed that none of the 200,000 starter homes promised in the 2015 Conservative manifesto had been built[22]. Below are Britain's nine regions highlighted in the 2023 House Price Index. Can you match them up to their respective average property price?

I. East Midlands

2. South East

3. Yorkshire and the Humber

4. North East

5. London

6. West Midlands

7. South West

8. East of England

9. North West

A. £351,898

B. £523,325

C. £246,092

D. £156,912

E. £394,543

F. £211,759

G. £326,035

H. £245,132

I. £203,635

WHAT A LOAD OF AWFUL CUTS

In 2010, George Osborne set out an emergency budget that the Institute for Fiscal Studies pointed out would make the biggest cuts to public services spending since the Second World War. Osborne had said the budget would protect 'the most vulnerable in society' but research in 2020 revealed that actually it was poorer – and dominantly Labour-run councils – who faced the biggest cuts (of the 50 councils worst hit by austerity, 28 were Labour-run while only 6 were Conservative).[23] Here are ten of the councils worst hit by austerity[24] – can you locate them on the map?

Camden   Salford

Gateshead   Slough

Hammersmith & Fulham   South Tyneside

Kensington & Chelsea   Westminster

Oldham   Wigan

LOCKDOWN PARTY SHOPPING LIST

Can you find the below ingredients for a secret shindig where social distancing is entirely optional?

Vodka
Party hats
Karaoke machine
Pinata
Prawn ring

Beer pong
Toga
Glowsticks
Disco ball
Condoms

```
I  B  A  E  J  G  P  W  V  V  K  O  B  X  M  Z  U  J  A  V  Q  Y  P
C  T  E  D  V  T  S  T  D  O  Z  K  R  W  F  H  Q  X  B  X  V  A  I
P  E  Z  E  G  S  Y  X  C  W  D  U  C  V  Y  K  C  W  J  T  A  C  N
Q  N  X  C  R  R  F  G  W  T  O  K  W  G  F  X  V  O  V  K  I  S  A
B  I  M  V  R  P  T  N  K  W  G  H  A  G  J  T  R  T  N  B  T  K  T
E  H  B  W  X  I  O  O  L  Q  H  S  X  N  S  N  X  U  P  D  A  P  A
Y  C  R  Z  R  T  C  N  G  X  X  V  C  I  Z  S  P  Q  O  P  O  S  Z
O  A  R  F  A  O  F  G  G  A  B  L  A  U  S  R  B  L  E  U  F  M  N
Z  M  F  W  C  C  M  G  S  C  E  O  G  L  O  W  S  T  I  C  K  S  S
I  E  W  U  J  H  L  B  O  Y  H  H  W  U  J  T  F  H  C  E  E  X  Z
T  K  I  H  D  S  T  A  H  Y  T  R  A  P  C  D  L  L  H  Y  X  J  P
O  O  R  K  Y  D  J  X  M  X  H  K  G  N  I  R  N  W  A  R  P  B  H
O  A  S  V  R  S  P  Z  R  L  O  Q  Q  G  L  L  A  B  O  C  S  I  D
B  R  C  Y  V  V  H  A  S  M  T  E  P  X  M  P  D  E  Q  I  B  G  L
N  A  W  E  B  X  J  G  D  X  E  U  R  N  X  L  F  Y  S  P  R  E  T
Z  K  T  F  C  L  G  B  C  K  E  J  I  N  S  N  J  L  O  T  L  R  Y
```

DOMINIC RAAB'S GEOGRAPHY CHALLENGE

Remember that time Dominic confused the Irish sea with the Red Sea[25] and didn't seem to understand that there's a bit of water between Dover and Calais[26]? Well, now he needs some help filling in his Atlas. Can you name the ten numbered countries on the map below?

HOW TO LOSE A BILLION POUNDS IN SIX MONTHS

Unless your surname is Sunak, a billion pounds sounds like quite a lot of money, so it was a bit of a shock in 2011 when the coalition government took that amount and spent it bombing the shit out of Libya. How much do you know about the fourth-biggest country in Africa?

I. What is the name of Libya's capital city?

A: Benghazi
B: Al Bayda
C: Tripoli
D: Ajdabiya

2. In 1969 Libya became a republic when King Idris I (the first, and only monarch of Libya) was overthrown by which unhinged psychopath politician?

A: Hosni Mubarak
B: Zine El Abidine Ben Ali
C: Ali Abdullah Saleh
D: Muammar Gaddafi

3. One of Libya's most famous landmarks is the three-hundred-foot Waw an Namus, but what is it?

A: Waterfall
B: Volcano
C: Temple
D: Canyon

4. What was unique about Libya's flag from 1977 to 2011?

A: It was the world's only purple flag
B: It was a square, rather than a rectangle
C: It was the only flag to depict a living person's face
D: It was the only flag that was just one colour and had no design

5. Lastly, can you place Libya on a map of North Africa?

TORY NAME GENERATOR

Ever wondered how pompous your name would be if you were a Tory? Use your first initial and birth month to find out!

FIRST NAME (MALE)

A – Sebastian
B – Tobias
C – Atticus
D – Bartholomew
E – Thaddeus
F – Jasper
G – Hugo
H – Julian
I – Crispin
J – Balthazar
K – Llewellyn
L – Rafe
M – Augustus
N – Percival
O – Hector
P – Timothy
Q – Walter
R – Peregrine
S – Herbert
T – Maximilian
U – Horatio
V – Clement
W – Ignatius
X – Merlin
Y – Godfrey
Z – Oswald

FIRST NAME (FEMALE)

A – Clementine
B – Artemis
C – Rosamund
D – Persephone
E – Helena
F – Hyacinth
G – Astrid
H – Ophelia
I – Fenella
J – Allegra
K – Camilla
L – Felicity
M – Evangeline
N – Aurelia
O – Vivienne
P – Beatrice
Q – Rosalind
R – Henrietta
S – Octavia
T – Marguerite
U – Jocasta
V – Annabel
W – Gwendolen
X – Penelope
Y – Portia
Z – Arabella

SURNAME

JANUARY	Fotherington-Beauchamp III
FEBRUARY	Cholmondeley-Wadsworth
MARCH	Humphrey-Harrington-Wellington
APRIL	Winthrop, Warden of Wessex
MAY	Montague
JUNE	Chamberlain-Mercer
JULY	Buckingham-Wentworth
AUGUST	Tudor
SEPTEMBER	Smythe-Smythe-Smythe
OCTOBER	Heathcliffe-Tennyson
NOVEMBER	Kipling-Berkley-Kensington-Spencer
DECEMBER	Keats, Custodian of the Royal Charter of Ravens

MY TORY NAME IS

Hugo chamberlain Mercer

Camila Fotherington
Keate Custodian of the
Royal Ravens

45

COLOURING CHALLENGE – PICTURESQUE BRITISH COASTAL SCENE

Here's a British seaside scene for you to colour in. It's a sunny day but there don't appear to many people paddling... perhaps it's a bit choppy.

CRAYONS REQUIRED:

Blue (sky)   **Yellow** (sun, sand)   **Dark brown** (sea)

KEEPING UP WITH THE SUNAKS

According to the 2023 Sunday Times Rich List, Rishi Sunak and Akshata Murty have a small personal fortune of – wait for it – £529 million. Using the figures from that same list, are the following wealthy people richer or poorer?

Ed Sheeran

Alan Sugar

Paul McCartney and Nancy Shevell

Simon Cowell

J.K. Rowling

Daniel Levy

King Charles III

James Dyson

Mike Ashley

Elton John

TRACTOR PORN

When Tory MP Neil Parish had the whip removed in April 2022 for watching pornography in the House of Commons, he initially claimed that he'd actually been looking at tractors. Since he's probably not got much going on since resigning, here are some steamy pictures to get him – and anybody else with a thing for farm machinery – hot under the collar. (If you're reading this book in public, perhaps save this bit for when you're on your own).

PARTY GAME – 'EARN' A TORY PEERAGE

There are three ways to get a seat in the House of Lords. You can either:

| Be an upstanding member of society | Be born into vast wealth | Give the Tories sack loads of cash[27] |

So here's a fun party game to replicate the thrill of receiving a peerage simply because you can afford it.

HOW TO PLAY:

On strips of paper, write down the donation amounts below and place them face down on a surface. Take it in turns with your fellow Tories to take a piece of paper to top up your donation total. First to reach one million pounds wins and is on their way to the House of Lords (as soon as you've deposited the cash in a secure offshore account).

£1,000	£40,000	£85,000
£3,000	£45,000	£90,000
£5,000	£50,000	£95,000
£10,000	£55,000	£100,000
£15,000	£60,000	£150,000
£20,000	£65,000	£200,000
£25,000	£70,000	£250,000
£30,000	£75,000	£300,000
£35,000	£80,000	£500,000

TO THE REFRIGERATOR!

Uh-oh! Journalists are asking difficult questions and Boris Johnson needs to retreat to his state-of-the-art command centre as quickly as possible. Can you help him sprint to the refrigerator before he's forced to give a direct answer?

SAY SOMETHING NICE ABOUT MARGARET THATCHER

Margaret Thatcher may no longer be with us, but that doesn't mean we can't say nice things about her. Here are some statements with space for you to fill in the blanks with kind words about our beloved former PM.

I think Margaret Thatcher was:

....

Her best quality was:

....

She will mostly be remembered for:

....

If I could spend ten minutes with her, I would say:

....

and I hope wherever she is, that she:

....

FIND THE TORY

How many of our all-time favourite Tories can you find
in this rather terrifying wordsearch?

Mark Francois
Jonathan Gullis
Peter Bone
Andrea Jenkyns
Andrew Bridgen

Bill Cash
Kemi Badinoch
Steve Baker
Amber Rudd
Christopher Chope

```
V  C  K  U  N  N  J  V  V  D  C  C  P  W  R  S  H  B  R  C  H  Y  V
K  H  E  R  R  H  U  O  R  E  S  J  F  E  X  I  I  Y  D  C  S  W  Q
X  R  M  I  V  S  Y  L  N  C  G  P  X  R  T  Z  X  R  C  A  F  A  Q
A  I  I  W  A  A  E  F  O  A  P  P  V  S  C  E  U  X  V  C  J  N  Z
S  S  B  X  P  C  C  L  R  P  T  G  Z  N  W  P  R  D  Q  R  P  D  D
I  T  A  X  A  L  X  B  C  Z  V  H  Y  Y  W  A  J  B  Z  S  T  R  Q
O  O  D  P  X  L  R  J  K  A  I  F  A  K  P  E  R  P  O  W  X  E  D
C  P  I  G  G  I  R  X  L  H  R  S  W  N  Z  I  F  P  S  N  H  W  V
N  H  N  Y  T  B  G  K  H  L  Y  R  T  E  G  Y  A  T  P  Q  E  B  R
A  E  O  L  T  M  P  C  N  V  G  E  Y  J  I  U  T  L  T  P  O  R  L
R  R  C  L  I  W  Y  M  Z  G  J  M  S  A  A  G  L  C  L  U  B  I  O
F  C  H  K  G  V  B  Y  E  D  T  X  N  E  B  R  H  L  Q  L  Y  D  P
K  H  Q  Z  F  C  R  S  D  U  J  I  T  R  N  I  I  F  I  B  B  G  B
R  O  E  S  T  E  V  E  B  A  K  E  R  D  I  B  E  S  V  S  L  E  L
A  P  D  L  E  V  D  F  F  R  G  N  Y  N  U  I  W  U  P  L  Z  N  Q
M  E  N  C  W  R  X  F  K  H  J  S  Y  A  M  B  E  R  R  U  D  D  F
```

THE HIGH HORSE

Not a Tory voter? Here's an extremely high horse for you to complete. Simply connect the body to the hooves to complete your moral superiority.

THIS MIGHT HURT A LITTLE

In 2010, the year David Cameron's Tory government came to power, the waiting list for NHS services was 2.5 million. That waiting list has increased every year since, and in May 2023 stood at 7.5 million.[28] Below, we've made up five patients – they each have a body part that needs attending to. Can you figure out from the clue which ailing body part matches each person?

PEOPLE

Emily
Brenda
Kendal
Hassan
Adanna

BODY PARTS

knee
kidney
womb
lung
eye

CLUES

This person's name begins with the same letter as the body part that ails them.

This person's ailing body part is one letter fewer than the letters in their name.

If you put the people in alphabetical order, and the body parts in alphabetical order, the person whose name comes first alphabetically has an ailment involving the body part that comes last alphabetically.

This person's name has a repeat of a vowel. Their ailing body part also has a repeat of a vowel.

This person's name is exactly double the letters of the ailing body part.

SPOT THE TORY STRONGHOLD

It's important to know when you're in an area with a huge Tory majority, so you can A) get out as quickly as possible, and B) loudly express your support for the European Union while you do so. Below are twenty constituencies. Ten recorded the largest Tory majorities at the 2019 general election[29], but they're mixed in with the ten safest Labour seats. Can you separate the Tory strongholds from the leftie safe havens?

Bethnal Green and Bow

Bootle

Boston and Skegness

Brentwood and Ongar

Camberwell and Peckham

Castle Point

Clacton

East Ham

Garston and Halewood

Hackney North and Stoke Newington

Hackney South and Shoreditch

Knowsley

Lewisham, Deptford

Liverpool, Riverside

Louth and Horncastle

Maldon

North East Cambridgeshire

Raleigh and Wickford

South Holland and the Deepings

South Staffordshire

TORY MAJORITY	LABOUR MAJORITY

JOIN THE DOTS

It's Friday night and the lights are low, but who is this waltzing their way onstage at the Conservative Party Conference? You May (ahem) have to join the dots to find out...

TORY PUB QUIZ: ROUND TWO

Here are ten more questions about what the
Tories have been up to, those busy, busy bees.

1. What was the name of Rishi Sunak's scheme aimed at getting people back into restaurants as the UK came out of lockdown in 2020?

A: Eat Out to Help Out
B: Dosh 4 Nosh
C: Grub-a-Pub-Dub
D: Thou Shalt Have a Dishy, From a Little Rishi

2. In 2015, then-London mayor Boris Johnson said (rather unconvincingly) that he would do what in order to stop the construction of a third runway at Heathrow?[30]

A: Cancel any construction contracts related to the project
B: Block access to the airport with his car
C: Lie down in front of bulldozers
D: Piss in the cement mixers

3. In April 2023 Andrew Bridgen was suspended from the Conservative Party for comparing Covid-19 vaccines to what?[31]

A: The persecution of Jesus
B: Genocide
C: The Holocaust
D: Slavery

59

4. In 2016 the Campaign Against Arms Trade claimed that under David Cameron, the UK had sold weapons worth £5.6 billion to which country?[32]

A: Iran
B: Israel
C: Yemen
D: Saudi Arabia

5. Which Tory MP became the shortest-serving education secretary of all time in 2022, resigning from the post after just forty-eight hours?

A: Kit Malthouse
B: Michelle Donelan
C: Damian Hinds
D: Gillian Keegan

6. In 2014, a group of leading Anglican bishops, Methodists and Quakers wrote an open letter blaming David Cameron's government for an unprecedented rise in what?[33]

A: Hate crimes
B: Food banks
C: Anti-religious sentiment
D: Homelessness

7. During the 8 March 2019 edition of the BBC's Politics Live, wannabe tough guy / angry hobbit Mark Francois had an incredibly awkward staredown with which novelist following an argument about Brexit?[34]

A: Ian McEwan
B: Neil Gaiman
C: Helen Fielding
D: Will Self

8. Which former cricketer (and staunch Brexiteer) was elevated to the House of Lords by Boris Johnson in July 2020?

A: Mike Gatting
B: Ian Botham
C: Mike Atherton
D: Geoffrey Boycott

9. The series of events that led to Boris Johnson's eventual downfall arguably started nine months earlier when party whips were instructed not to back the Standards Committee over a thirty-day suspension for which MP?

A: Peter Aldous
B: Steve Baker
C: Priti Patel
D: Owen Paterson

10. At the height of the Covid Pandemic in 2020, the government supported the 'Clap for Our Carers' movement, though some said they'd prefer adequate pay and/or PPE. On which night of the week did it take place?

A: Tuesday
B: Wednesday
C: Thursday
D: Friday

CREATE YOUR OWN TORY CABINET

Ever wanted to experience the thrill of picking your very own Tory cabinet? Well now you can! From the options below, can you create a strong, stable government and secure a prosperous future, free of sleaze and scandal?

Prime Minister

....

Deputy Prime Minister

....

Chancellor

....

Home Secretary

....

Foreign Secretary

....

Education Secretary

....

Health Secretary

....

Leader of the House of Commons

....

Montgomery Burns

Darth Vader

Ming the Merciless

The Demon Headmaster

Larry the Cat

Frank Spencer

A Dalek

Joffrey Baratheon

The Wet Bandits

Hannibal Lecter

Emperor Palpatine

A potato

Hans Gruber

Richard Hillman

Freddy Krueger

Lord Sauron

The Shark from *Jaws*

Skeletor

J.R Ewing

Tim Nice-But-Dim

Skeletor

A bowl of porridge

Kwasi Kwarteng

I THINK WE SHOULD
SEE OTHER CURRENCIES

The value of the pound has seen some serious slumps under the Tories. John Major's government famously had to withdraw sterling from the ERM in 1992 because the pound was no longer strong enough to participate[35], Liz Truss's mini budget saw the pound fall to its lowest ever level against the dollar[36], and the less said about Brexit the better[37]...

Before deciding whether you want a different type of tender in the UK, first see if you can match the following currencies to their respective countries.

1. Zloty

2. Rand

3. Forint

4. Yen

5. Dong

6. Lev

7. Rial

8. Krona

9. Baht

10. Lek

A. Japan

B. Bulgaria

C. South Africa

D. Thailand

E. Vietnam

F. Iran

G. Poland

H. Hungary

I. Albania

J. Sweden

TORIES BY NUMBERS

The following numbers all relate to Tory rule since 2010.
Can you match them up with the correct statement?

I. 40

2. 350,000,000

3. 3.13

4. 126

5. 57

6. 44

7. 1,000,000,000

8. 62

9. 800,000

10. 253

A. Number of fixed penalty notices handed out by the Metropolitan Police during the 2022 so-called partygate scandal.

B. Amount (in pounds) that former BBC chairman Richard Sharp helped to arrange for Boris Johnson.

C. Length of time (in days) that Liz Truss spent as prime minister.

D. Number of new hospitals pledged by Boris Johnson in the 2019 Tories' 2019 election manifesto.

E. The amount (in pounds) promised to the DUP over five years to help prop up Theresa May's minority government in 2018.

F. Percentage of his £320,000 fee for appearing on I'm a Celebrity... Get Me Out of Here! that Matt Hancock donated to charity.

G. The number of Lib Dem MPs who joined the coalition government in 2010.

H. Amount (in pounds) that the infamous 'Brexit bus' claimed the UK sent to the EU every week, and which could instead go to the NHS.

I. Total number of resignations (ministers, private secretaries, trade envoys, and vice-chairmen) from Boris Johnson's government that forced his hand and led to his resignation in July 2022.

J. Distance (in miles) from 10 Downing Street to Barnard Castle.

TORY TRUE OR FALSE: ROUND ONE

Some people might argue that certain Tories have a pretty hard time differentiating between the truth, and complete and utter bollocks, so see if you can fare any better. Below are ten statements about the Tories, but are they true or false?

1. In the run-up to the 2019 general election, Lee Anderson was caught on camera getting one of his friends to pretend to be an anti-Labour swing voter after forgetting that his microphone was still on.

2. In 2022, ex-Tory minister John Redwood suggested that severe NHS bed shortages could be solved by simply adding more.

3. In February 2011, Transport Secretary Justine Greening fell into the River Trent during the opening of a kayak club in Nottingham.

4. In 2017 a property owned by Jeremy Hunt was deemed 'unsuitable for human inhabitation' after a tenant was hospitalised with a severe respiratory infection.

5. In 2018 Tory backbencher Christopher Chope objected to a bill which aimed to make upskirting a criminal offence.

6. Following the exit poll results at the 2019 general election, a Tory candidate in Hertfordshire rolled a cigarette using a £20 note, and then lost by just thirteen votes.

7. While serving breakfast at a shelter in London shortly after becoming prime minister, Rishi Sunak asked a homeless man if he worked in business.

8. Penny Mordaunt paid her way through sixth form by working as a magician's assistant.

9. A 2006 biography of Ted Heath claimed that the former PM once put an injured pigeon out of its misery by snapping its neck, but accidentally decapitated it in the process.

10. While on his honeymoon in 2014, Jonathan Gullis was taken to hospital after being bitten by a stray cat.

HELP DAVID CAMERON FIND HIS SHED

The date is 24 June 2016 and David Cameron needs to scuttle off to the comfort of his bespoke writing shed. Can you help him find his way while avoiding the responsibilities of a competent world leader?

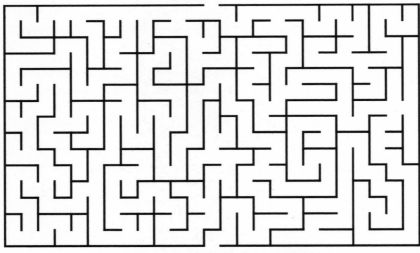

FREE GIFT! CUT-OUT-AND-KEEP LIFE-SIZED RISHI SUNAK

This 1:1 scale Rishi Sunak can be used as a bookmark or for scaring squirrels away from bird feeders. Enjoy!

FIND THE CHEESE!

Despite being PM for a whole six weeks, Liz Truss will forever be best known for saying 'That. Is. A. Disgrace' in relation to a (possibly completely made up) stat that the UK imports two-thirds of its cheese.[38] In honour of Liz's incredible political legacy, can you find the following types of cheese in this wordsearch?

Cheddar
Stilton
Gouda
Brie
Manchego
Camembert
Edam

Parmesan
Mozzarella
Feta
Gorgonzola
Roquefort
Emmental
Munster

```
P  M  E  S  D  P  G  Q  V  G  F  K  M  O  A  R  A  D  D  E  H  C  V
M  A  L  U  X  B  D  X  R  F  O  T  R  M  D  Q  P  R  S  B  S  N  S
C  N  F  M  A  D  E  J  C  R  H  R  G  X  O  K  O  K  Q  L  E  F  C
D  C  Y  Y  V  E  A  E  H  X  Z  B  G  T  B  Z  J  C  U  Q  C  W  V
Y  H  X  D  E  X  B  K  G  R  Z  U  Y  O  G  Z  Z  Q  M  Q  I  E  B
S  E  Y  Y  C  A  D  V  S  L  O  C  B  X  N  H  T  A  T  B  R  E  Z
T  G  U  H  Q  K  I  O  R  Y  C  Q  W  R  N  Z  C  U  R  O  A  A  C
I  O  F  E  T  A  Y  K  L  B  Z  P  U  B  I  M  O  D  E  E  J  U  T
L  G  G  S  N  A  S  E  M  R  A  P  T  E  V  E  T  L  S  W  L  A  Y
T  P  A  U  C  U  U  G  H  M  C  U  J  D  F  E  W  I  A  D  R  L  C
O  O  D  M  W  B  T  K  Z  V  C  T  B  C  S  O  F  Q  H  A  V  G  A
N  Q  L  S  J  Z  Y  T  R  E  B  M  E  M  A  C  R  A  D  C  O  D  P
K  A  C  G  J  S  P  I  B  L  A  T  N  E  M  M  E  T  U  I  R  B  Y
R  X  N  X  H  K  S  B  B  L  H  H  F  K  U  T  O  B  O  E  F  B  S
I  H  R  R  N  P  P  U  G  H  U  T  G  O  U  D  A  N  X  D  K  L  V
K  I  B  Z  T  E  Q  C  M  U  N  S  T  E  R  L  F  O  X  G  P  F  L
```

TORIES: MASTERS OF THE LUCRATIVE SECOND JOB

Research conducted by Sky News and Tortoise Media in January 2023 – better known as The Westminster Accounts – revealed that of the £17.1m earned by MPs from second jobs since the 2019 general election, £15.2m of it went into the pockets of Conservatives.[39] Some people might say: good on them. Others might say: that might cause a conflict of interest and do they definitely have enough time to do the first job if they have a second? Whichever side you fall on, can you match the following Tories to the amount they earned?

1. Boris Johnson

2. Nadine Dorries

3. David Davis

4. Chris Grayling

5. Owen Paterson

6. Geoffrey Cox

7. Theresa May

8. Fiona Bruce

9. Sajid Javid

10. John Redwood

A. £711,749

B. £2,191,387

C. £181,556

D. £209,227

E. £692,438

F. £1,064,785

G. £361,566

H. £224,487

I. £191,316

J. £2,550,876

THE LIZ TRUSSWORD

Here's a crossword about Liz Truss, which in all likelihood
will take longer to complete than her entire premiership.

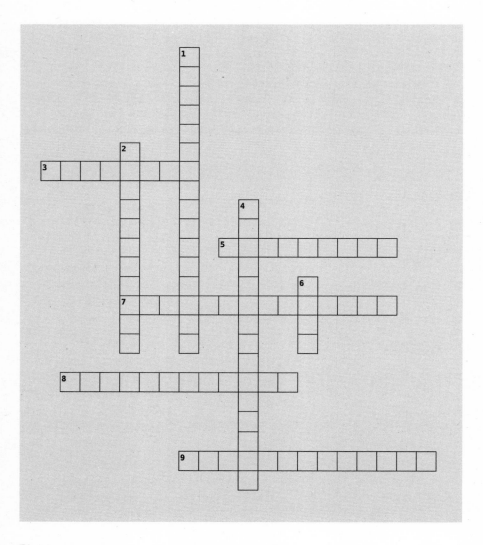

DOWN

1. Political party that she was an active member of prior to becoming a Tory in 1996.

2. Complete the classic Liz Truss quote: 'In December, I'll be in Beijing, opening up new ....'

3. On 9 August 2022 Liz Truss told a hustings crowd 'We need to get on with delivering the small modular nuclear reactors which we produce here in Derbyshire'. Which county was she actually in?

6. What is Liz Truss's actual first name? (Elizabeth is her middle name.)

ACROSS

4. Royal residence where Liz Truss met the Queen just two days before her death. (Imagine living for ninety-six years and one of the last things you see is Liz Truss...)

5. On the 4 September 2022 edition of Sunday with Laura Kuenssberg, which comedian insisted that Liz Truss was very clear in her answers and that he was 'very right-wing'?

7. On her way to winning the 2022 Tory leadership contest, Liz Truss said the 'jury's out' on whether which world leader was a friend or foe of the UK?

8. Russian foreign minister who described a 2022 conversation with Liz Truss as 'turning out like the conversation of a mute and a deaf person'.

9. Who served as Deputy Prime Minister under Liz Truss (for all of six weeks)?

GOOD MEMORIES

Below are fourteen things that the Tories have done since they
came to power in 2010, but can you put them into the order they happened?

1. Priti Patel resigns as international development secretary over unofficial meetings with Israelis.[40]

2. Kwasi Kwarteng's 'mini budget' that almost wiped out the British economy.[41]

3. Liam Fox resigns as defence secretary after letting a personal friend attend meetings that he wasn't cleared for.[42]

4. Amber Rudd resigns as home secretary, following strong criticism of her role in the treatment of Windrush generation migrants.[43]

5. Andrew Mitchell resigns for an incident at Downing Street which would later become known as 'Plebgate'.[44]

6. Government puts Dido Harding in charge of NHS Test and Trace.[45]

7. A biography by Lord Ashcroft alleges that David Cameron took part in a peculiar initiation ceremony involving a pig and a part of his anatomy.[46]

8. Nadhim Zahawi is sacked following an investigation into his tax affairs.[47]

9. The proroguing of Parliament, which is later ruled to be unlawful.[48]

10. Matt Hancock's caught-on-camera snog with Gina Coladangelo.[49]

11. Culture secretary Maria Miller resigns after two years of intense scrutiny over her parliamentary expenses claims.[50]

12. Proposals to increase tuition fees result in student riots outside Conservative Party headquarters in London.[51]

13. Home Office deploys 'go home' vans to areas of London with high immigrant populations.[52]

14. David Cameron announces EU referendum, which went famously well.[53]

JOIN THE DOTS

It's 2012 and this Tory has just unwittingly created the defining image of their political career. Join the dots to reveal who it is; there's no time to hang around!

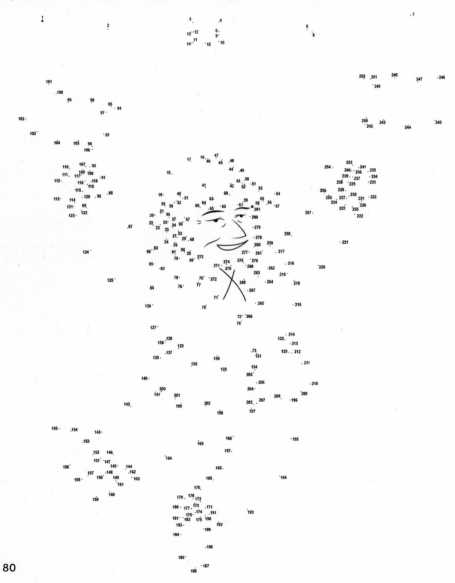

CREATE YOUR OWN BREXIT BUS

Ever fancied your very own Brexit bus? Here's a picture of one with space on the side for you to write the biggest, most outrageous lie you can think of.

RUBBISH TORY BOOKS

Some might say (not us) that certain Tories rarely pass up the chance of supplemental revenue streams. Lucky for them, publishers keep offering them deals, although we'd have thought 'people who want to read about history from the perspective of a millionaire hedge fund manager' is a fairly niche subset of readers. Can you match the following books to the Tories who wrote them?

1. The Victorians: Twelve Titans Who Forged Britain

2. The Angels of Lovely Lane

3. Churchill: How One Man Made History

4. Snakes and Ladders: Navigating the Ups and Downs of Politics

5. The Abuse of Power

6. Ghosts of Empire: Britain's Legacies in the Modern World

7. The Path to Power

8. The Devil's Tune

9. The Clematis Tree

10. Pandemic Diaries: The Inside Story of Britain's Battle Against Covid

A. Matt Hancock

B. Kwasi Kwarteng

C. Theresa May

D. Jacob Rees-Mogg

E. Nadine Dorries

F. Andrea Leadsom

G. Ann Widdecombe

H. Iain Duncan Smith

I. Margaret Thatcher

J. Boris Johnson

MEANINGLESS TORY SLOGANS

Let's be honest: the majority of political slogans are complete tosh,
and the Tories' chosen mottos are no exception. Can you find the
following mantras in the wordsearch below?

Vote for change
Forward, together
Strong and stable
Get Brexit done
Stop the boats

Build back better
Getting on with the job
Time for common sense
Global Britain
Big society

```
X  T  S  G  E  T  T  I  N  G  O  N  W  I  T  H  T  H  E  J  O  B  T
V  V  Y  E  X  D  J  T  X  S  S  R  R  R  M  P  G  D  F  O  G  R  X
T  O  E  D  H  K  I  A  P  K  Y  T  E  I  C  O  S  G  I  B  G  E  Q
S  T  N  S  C  H  B  L  O  A  O  G  H  I  M  G  U  S  K  J  V  T  N
T  E  O  M  E  E  W  X  Q  L  C  P  T  I  C  E  J  S  O  D  H  T  I
O  F  D  C  B  R  U  O  G  L  U  G  E  T  V  A  H  J  T  E  V  E  A
P  O  T  K  E  M  H  X  V  X  D  Z  G  C  D  N  N  H  N  D  L  B  T
T  R  I  E  S  N  E  S  N  O  M  M  O  C  R  O  F  E  M  I  T  K  I
H  C  X  P  P  D  U  V  L  Y  Y  C  T  T  A  D  S  I  P  L  G  C  R
E  H  E  Q  S  E  E  L  B  A  T  S  D  N  A  G  N  O  R  T  S  A  B
B  A  R  D  R  Y  O  L  P  J  N  R  R  F  J  W  C  J  M  M  A  B  L
O  N  B  A  E  Z  H  L  T  O  F  K  A  E  R  S  A  X  E  T  M  D  A
A  G  T  F  J  Z  A  M  K  R  W  U  W  Q  A  J  D  U  P  S  M  L  B
T  E  E  R  B  K  F  P  E  Y  L  O  R  F  J  S  U  Y  I  M  U  I  O
S  I  G  Y  D  L  E  I  C  L  O  U  O  D  G  Q  G  H  S  Y  B  U  L
I  Z  P  B  Y  Z  H  E  E  G  U  V  F  O  E  H  U  J  J  X  R  B  G
```

ELECTION NIGHT COLOURING FUN

Make election night even more exciting by colouring
in the constituencies as they come in! Requires:

1 x red crayon   1 x yellow crayon   (Blue crayon optional)

TORY TRUE OR FALSE: ROUND TWO

Here are ten more statements about Tory times,
but which are true, and which are false?

1. MP for Ashfield Lee Anderson claimed that would-be foodbank users could instead knock up nutritious meals for just thirty pence.

2. In 2016, police were called to Bournemouth Beach after Jacob Rees-Mogg used a fake £20 note to hire a deckchair.

3. Gavin Williamson was so scared of veteran Labour MP Denis Skinner that he once hid in a toilet cubicle for almost twenty minutes to avoid running into him.

4. In 1996, Ken Clarke was removed from a plane by Turkish police after being caught smoking a cigar in the toilet.

5. In 2019, Foreign Office minister Mark Field was suspended after grabbing a female climate protester by the neck.

6. In order to skip the queue at his local B&Q during the Covid pandemic, Tory backbencher Simon Fell told staff that he was there to make sure all safety procedures were being followed, before buying three tins of paint and a patio heater.

7. In 2011, Minister for Sport Hugh Robertson choked on an egg sandwich while showing VIPs around the London Olympic stadium, and was given the Heimlich manoeuvre by Lennox Lewis.

8. During an episode of Good Evening Britain in 2018 Danny Dyer called former PM David Cameron a 'twat' during a discussion which included Jeremy Corbyn and Pamela Anderson.

9. In 2017 Michael Fabricant appeared on Channel 4's First Dates.

10. In 2018, Kemi Badenoch admitted that she once hacked Harriet Harman's official website, adding a fake blog post announcing that the Labour MP was backing Boris Johnson's bid to become London mayor.

THE PRETENTIOUS BLUSTER OF BORIS JOHNSON

One of the key skills Tory politicians possess is throwing out phrases and words which haven't been used in everyday language for hundreds of years. The former PM Boris Johnson has used all of the following terms during his political career, but can you match them to their definitions?

1. Gibbering rictus

2. Hogwhimpering

3. Maenads

4. Poule de luxe

5. Hypothalamus

6. Ziggurats

7. Boondoggle

8. Hottentot

9. Swankpot

10. Popinjay

A. Antiquated term for a conceited person

B. Term used to describe someone who is open-mouthed with fear

C. The part of the brain that stimulates sex drive

D. A wasteful, fraudulent, or unnecessary project

E. French slang for an expensive prostitute

F. Archaic term for a parrot. Can be used to describe a talkative person

G. Adjective for extreme drunkenness

H. The female followers of the Greek god of wine, Dionysus. Known for their drunken behaviour

I. An ancient Mesopotamian temple

J. Seventeenth-century racial term to describe nomadic South African pastoralists

USE PREDICTIVE TEXT TO WRITE YOUR OWN TORY MANIFESTO

The 2019 Conservative party's manifesto was just 59 pages compared to Labour's 105 and the Liberal Democrats' 96. Concise ... or lazy? In a completely unrelated game, don't bother giving time and thought to complete the below pledges, use predictive text to do so instead.

I will tackle immigration by sending asylum seekers to

....

Potholes will be a thing of the past, as I will fill them with

....

In the case of another pandemic, I would order everybody to

....

If people are caught protesting, I will authorise the police to

....

If one of my ministers breaks the ministerial code, they will be

....

To get the economy back on track, I will sell off

....

I will use the £350-million-a-week that we're not sending to the EU to fund

....

If accused of lying to the House, I will claim that I was simply

....

I will award a knighthood to

....

I will tackle homelessness by forcing rough sleepers to

....

And finally, my campaign slogan is

....

BRITANNIA UNHINGED

2012 saw the release of *Britannia Unchained: Global Lessons for Growth and Prosperity*, a book about the state of modern Britain written by – wait for it – Priti Patel, Liz Truss, Kwasi Kwarteng, Dominic Raab, and Chris Skidsmore. Below are five inspirational quotes from the book, but some words have been removed. Can you fill in the blanks?

I. Once they enter the workplace, the British are among the _____ in the world. We work among the lowest hours, we retire early and our productivity is poor.

A: Most slovenly
B: Worst idlers
C: Least motivated
D: Biggest procrastinators

2. But why would a student put themselves through the hard graft when the jobs are open to those who have managed to spend their university days _____ as well as the library?

A: Frequenting nightclubs
B: Lying in bed
C: Endlessly browsing social media
D: In the pub

3. We must stop bailing out the reckless, avoiding all risk, and rewarding
_____.

A: Laziness
B: The uninspired
C: Failure
D: The uneducated

4. If indifferent parenting and mediocre schooling have contributed to an erosion
of the British work ethic, some argue it has been further exacerbated by an
increasingly pervasive _____.

A: Left-wing press
B: Lack of motivation
C: Celebrity culture
D: Woke hive mind

5. Instead, attracted by the idea of longer _____ for future generations some
in Britain want their children to sit back and enjoy the fruits of their prosperity.

A: Working hours
B: Lie-ins
C: Sick days
D: Tax breaks

WHO AM I?

Below are five Tories, with three clues each as to their identity.
Can you work out who they are? For ultimate bragging rights,
see if you can crack the case from just the first clue.

???

1.
— I am the Member of Parliament for South Staffordshire.
— I was Education Secretary when a disastrous algorithm downgraded thousands of A-level results in 2020.
— I was rewarded with a knighthood in 2022.

2.
— I am the Member of Parliament for Mid Bedfordshire.
— In 2021 I landed the role of Culture Secretary and (unsuccessfully) tried to privatise Channel 4.
— In 2012 I had the whip removed after appearing on *I'm a Celebrity ... Get Me Out Of Here!*. I finished eleventh.

3.
— I was the Member of Parliament for Buckingham from 1997 to 2019.
— I was the first MP since 1971 to become Speaker of the House of Commons without having first served as Deputy Speaker.
— After stepping down as Speaker in 2019, I briefly joined the Labour Party, but my years of Toryness came back to haunt me and I was suspended after a wide-ranging bullying investigation.[54]

4.

— I am the Member of Parliament for Witham.
— My grandparents emigrated from India to Uganda, and my parents emigrated from Uganda to the UK.
— Whilst serving as Home Secretary I introduced a points-based immigration system and laid the groundwork for the government's notorious Rwanda policy. I have been known to smirk at inappropriate moments.[55]

5.

— I am the Member of Parliament for West Suffolk.
— While serving as Culture Secretary, I launched an app named after myself.[56] It was not very popular.
— I ate a camel's penis for money.

JOIN THE DOTS

A former prime minister is enjoying their favourite snack, but who is it?
Join the dots to find out!

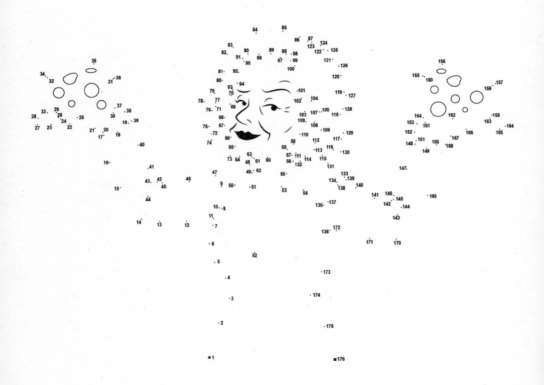

QUESTIONABLE ARMS EXPORTS

The following wordsearch contains ten countries
that have two things in common:

1. They've appeared on the UK's human rights countries of concern list since the Tories came to power in 2010.
2. We've sold them a shitload of weapons.[57]

Can you find them all?

Myanmar	Somalia	Yemen
Pakistan	Saudi Arabia	Zimbabwe
Russia	Venezuela	Afghanistan
	Mali	

```
L T X K Q R A F Z I D M M A E W B A B M I Z Z
Z E G V E J R Q S P E A M F A O Z Q A T C C L
Q D C O Z F A Z Y Q J L W G A I T L U R B G Y
E E D S B I M S D N P I C H W M U P Z N G N W
B V B B X G N U Z U W R A A Q S D A E E H G U
C C B B B Z A C M U W D O N M R K K G A W W E
P I E G W I Y Z L A X Y T I S U K I N G W J P
H G B U L H M N T E M V A S U Y O S W L X P G
B V K I G K E R T Z V K K T R A W T B N E U X
R E T M K N E M E Y K Z F A C O J A Y T D Z Z
C C J T F F G Z O I A D I N R D Y N I B D O U
S A U D I A R A B I A L I Q W F I S W Q Y B L
P K M D X R M D E E A I S S U R B Y R N E B W
P K D D U S C Q Y X R P D Y C V S R B X E Q B
C A I U X K Y A I V U L H S K S O M A L I A L
Z A N V E N E Z U E L A H W Q Y L O K V Y Z R
```

CREATE YOUR OWN TORY SCANDAL

Fancy your very own Tory scandal? Use your initials to find out why you're being cancelled by the anti-establishment woke mob.

I ....

A   Was caught having sex with ....
B   Accepted illicit donations from ....
C   Was accused of bribing ....
D   Had a fist fight with ....
E   Enjoyed an all-expenses-paid holiday with ....
F   Was spotted by a member of the public doing naked backflips with ....
G   Was photographed in a jacuzzi with ....
H   Reversed their car over ....
I   Admitted to having an affair with ....
J   Threw an egg at ....
K   Was caught making derogatory comments about ....
L   Cooked and ate ....
M   Urinated on ....
N   Designed an erotic cake depicting ....
O   Impregnated ....
P   Committed bigamy by marrying ....
Q   Was caught on camera French kissing ....
R   Caught a sexually-transmitted disease from ....
S   Shared a bath with ....
T   Awarded a PPE contract to ....
U   Emptied a jar of Marmite all over ....
V   Entered into a money laundering scheme with ....
W   Drove my car into ....
X   Eloped to Portugal with ....
Y   Ordered a colony of ants to attack ....
Z   Was caught buying a bag of cocaine from ....

A Sir Lindsay Hoyle
B Jacob Rees-Mogg's nanny
C Ant and Dec
D Black Rod
E A family of pigeons
F Keir Starmer
G Prince Andrew
H A waxwork of Simon Cowell
I Nicola Sturgeon's husband
J Michael Fabricant's wig
K A carrier bag full of horse meat
L Nadine Dorries
M Gary Lineker
N The Somerset Gimp
O The Archbishop of Canterbury
P A cardboard cut-out of Winston Churchill
Q A Nigerian prince
R Dominic Cummings
S Larry the cat
T Michael Green and Corrine Stockheath
U Dido Harding
V An out-of-work Phillip Schofield lookalike
W Nigel Farage
X Lord Alan Sugar
Y An overweight man with a nappy fetish
Z Jeremy Corbyn

PARTY OR NO PARTY?

During the Covid pandemic, Boris Johnson was placed in the impossible position of having to work out what does and doesn't constitute a full-blown rave. Below are ten scenarios, but can you work out which are parties, and which are the socially-distanced actions of a responsible prime minister?

1. You're alone in a room with Rishi Sunak. He is sitting three metres away and offering his thoughts on the Bank of England's latest inflation statement.

2. You are second from the back in a forty-six-man conga line. The person behind you throws up and a chunk of carrot lands on your shoe.

3. You are sitting alone in the Downing Street garden, reflecting on the terrible loss of life caused by the Covid pandemic.

4. Michael Gove has his arse well and truly wedged in the photocopier. You and sixteen other people gather round and laugh at him until the fire brigade arrives.

5. A colleague emails to ask if their department can have a small drinks reception after work. You decline the request as it's important to set a good example while lockdown rules are in place.

6. Dominic Cummings is doing the funky chicken on your desk and encouraging people to drink vodka from a shoe. Somebody throws a takeaway pizza like a frisbee and it hits a ceiling fan, showering everyone in ham and pineapple.

7. During a visit to a local hospital, you pay tribute to the hard work of staff, and reassure them that their wellbeing is at the forefront of your mind. You are wearing a mask and maintaining a safe distance at all times.

8. An extremely flustered Matt Hancock emerges from the Downing Street broom cupboard and gives you a high five. He is not wearing any trousers and you can't help but notice that his hand is sticky.

9. It's been a long week and you want to let your hair down. You crack open a bottle of wine and settle down to watch television with members of your own household.

10. Karaoke is in full swing and the crowd is going wild for Rishi Sunak's rousing rendition of Bohemian Rhapsody. You take a quick break from shaving off a junior minister's eyebrows to piss through an open window. Larry the Cat – sitting directly below – is not best pleased.

VICTORIAN SHOPPING WITH JACOB REES-MOGG

Nanny has given Jacob Rees-Mogg permission to do some shopping, but he's not sure where to start on his local Victorian high street. Can you match the items on his list to the places most likely to stock them?

1. Snuff

2. Clove rocks

3. Castor oil

4. A silk bonnet

5. Pattern 1861 Enfield musketoon

6. Cloth

7. A tankard of mead

8. Half a bushel of milk

9. A shoulder of mutton

10. Four buttons and a packet of hair pins

A. Haberdashery

B. Milliner

C. Gunsmith

D. Draper

E. Butcher

F. Apothecary

G. Public house

H. Confectioner

I. Dairyman

J. Tobacconist

A NUMBER TWO IN NUMBER TEN

Larry the Cat has overdone it on the chunks in jelly and needs to visit the toilet. Can you help him navigate the maze below and take a huge steaming shit on the cabinet room table?

TALLER OR SHORTER THAN RISHI SUNAK?

The first thing world leaders think when they meet Rishi Sunak
is usually 'where the hell is he?' before looking down to see what appears
to be a ventriloquist's dummy tugging at their trouser leg.

In truth he stands at five feet and six inches, but are the following things
taller, or shorter than him?

Ten cans of Pringles

A 2022 Nissan Micra

Mother Teresa (when she was alive)

The Mona Lisa

Forty Big Macs

Two hundred Maltesers

The Venus de Milo

Three Fender Stratocaster guitars

An Olympic spec men's javelin

The Mars Curiosity Rover

#TORYSCMU –
ANAGRAMS ROUND TWO

1. **DWARFISM NO WORKER** (Two words). Official name for Rishi Sunak's Northern Ireland protocol deal, struck in 2023 despite repeated claims from the government that they'd already got Brexit 'done'.

2. **CULT TEE** (One word). Vegetable which famously outlasted Liz Truss during a livestream organised by the Daily Star.

3. **GLACIER PANELLIST** (Two words). Financial services company which became mired in a lobbying scandal involving David Cameron in 2021.[58]

4. **FLAMENCO LILAH** (Two words) Former Tory defence secretary who resigned in 2017 amid allegations of sexual harassment.[59]

5. **SILVIA JEMMY** (Two words). Disgraced TV personality that Boris Johnson falsely accused Keir Starmer of failing to prosecute.[60]

6. **CONVENIENTLY HELIOTROPISM** (Three words) Widely used term for measures introduced by Theresa May in 2012, aiming to make things as difficult as possible for people without leave to remain in the UK.[61]

7. **BEAKER VEST** (Two words). Tory MP referred to (by himself at least) as 'the hard man of Brexit'[62] despite looking like a cross between Louis Theroux and Walter the Softy.

8. **HOISTED WAFFLE** (Three words). While on the campaign trail for the 2017 general election, Theresa May revealed that running through these was the naughtiest thing she'd ever done.

9. **BOX FANTASIES** (Two words). One of the aliases that Grant Shapps was accused of using to promote an internet marketing firm.[63]

10. **COLE JETTY** (Two words). British comedian that left Liz Truss red-faced[64] after sarcastically telling Laura Kuenssberg that he thought she was very clear, and that he was very right-wing.

TORY CHANCELLORS CROSSWORD

It's no secret that 'Tory Chancellor' has one of the top turnover rates of any job in the UK, with six of them holding that red briefcase since the Conservatives came to power in 2010. The answers to this crossword are all Tory chancellors, including a handful of historic ones.

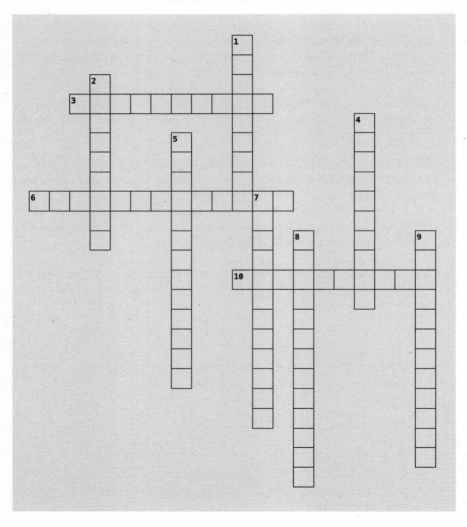

DOWN

1. (26 October 1989 – 28 November 1990) Margaret Thatcher's final chancellor, who has looked like a sixty-year-old man for the best part of forty years.

2. (27 May 1993 – 2 May 1997) Considered by some to be one of the 'good Tories' – and was the Father of the House for two years until his retirement from the Commons in 2019.

4. (13 February 2020 – 5 July 2022) Pint-sized chancellor who spent a large portion of his time in No 11 trying to convince people that it was safe to go out for Sunday lunch during the Covid pandemic – a move that was warmly welcomed by the virus itself.

5. (6 September 2022 – 14 October 2022) Appointed chancellor, crashed the economy, insisted he was going nowhere, then got sacked after just thirty-six days by his equally incompetent boss.

7. (28 November 1990 – 27 May 1993) A life peer and staunch Brexit supporter, who – due to his gigantic eyebrows – looks like a badly-stuffed taxidermy owl.

8. (13 July 2016 – 24 July 2019) Served as chancellor under Theresa May and led the group of MPs who helped to block Boris Johnson's 'no deal' Brexit plan in the Commons, losing the whip as a result.

9. (5 July 2022 – 6 September 2022) Distinctly unremarkable stint as chancellor, but would later come under scrutiny due to a seven-figure tax settlement.

ACROSS

3. (14 October 2022 – unknown) As of time of printing they're still in the job, but it's entirely plausible there might have been another three or four Tory chancellors since. His surname is often mispronounced on live TV.

6. (11 May 2010 – 13 July 2016) Responsible for the coalition government's austerity measures, and is famous for having a lot of jobs, even for a Tory.

10. (24 July 2019 – 13 February 2020) Mainly known for having a perfectly round head but has also served as Culture Secretary, Business Secretary, Home Secretary, and Health Secretary.

GUESS THE TORY FROM THE CHILD'S DRAWING

Here are four completely unofficial portraits of Tories past and present, but they've been drawn by children (special thanks to Jackson – eleven, and Serena – eight, and apologies for making you look at pictures of Tories at such a young age). Can you guess who they are?

I.

2.

3.

4.

TORY PUB QUIZ: ROUND THREE

One final round...

I. In December 2022 the Institute for Public Policy Research report claimed that people in the UK were becoming 'sicker and poorer', with a worsening health and wealth divide. Which region – according to the report – had been hit hardest?[65]

A: The North East
B: Cornwall
C: Northern Ireland
D: Scotland

2. Costs relating to the HS2 project have spiralled since 2010, with conservative estimates as of 2023 putting the project in the region of £40 billion.[66] Despite this, in November 2021 the government announced that the eastern leg had been scrapped, meaning the line would no longer visit which northern city?

A: Hull
B: Leeds
C: Liverpool
D: Bradford

3. In 2018 The Trussell Trust blamed what for a 52 per cent increase in food bank demand?[67]

A: Bedroom tax
B: Brexit
C: Rising food prices
D: Universal credit

4. In March 2023, which government minister sent out an email blaming the government's failure to stop small boat crossings on 'an activist blob of left-wing lawyers, civil servants and the Labour party'?[68]

A: Jacob Rees-Mogg
B Suella Braverman
C: Dominic Raab
D: James Cleverly

5. Which Tory foreign secretary was forced to apologise during a trip to China after mistakenly referring to his wife as Japanese?[69]

A: William Hague
B: Jeremy Hunt
C: Philip Hammond
D: Boris Johnson

6. After being appointed Tory party deputy chair in February 2023, Lee Anderson's first port of call was to call for the reintroduction of the death penalty. What claim did he make about it?[70]

A: That people who are sent to prison for a third time should be executed instead
B: That people would watch executions on the television just like Songs of Praise or Antiques Roadshow
C: Nobody has ever committed a crime after being executed
D: That he would be happy to personally carry out the executions

7. In April 2023, Liz Truss resurfaced for the first time since her stint in No 10 by giving a 'comeback' speech in Washington DC. What did she say was to blame for high taxes?[71]

A: Spiteful bankers
B: George Soros
C: Woke culture
D: Kwasi Kwarteng

8. Which Conservative life peer seemingly disappeared after being accused of recommending PPE Medpro via the so-called 'VIP lane', and then personally profiting from the deal?[72]

A: Michelle Mone
B: Karren Brady
C: Zac Goldsmith
D: Jo Johnson

9. What claim did ex Tory MP Michael Heseltine (notable in Margaret Thatcher and John Major's governments) make during an interview with Tatler magazine in November 2016?[73]

A: That aliens are real, and he'd seen one at a government facility
B: That he once strangled a dog to death
C: That John Major punched him in the face after he made a disrespectful comment about Edwina Currie
D: That he once walked in on Margaret Thatcher while she was using the toilet

10. In October 2018, which Conservative MP lost his temper and replied to a Twitter user demanding to know whether they'd insinuated that his wife was a prostitute in the Plymouth Herald Comments section?[74]

A: Rehman Chishti
B: David Davis
C: Damian Green
D: Johnny Mercer

FUCK THE TORIES:
ANSWERS

PAGES 8-9: AWFUL TORY VOTING RECORDS

1. **E.** Between 2013 – 2019, MP for North East Somerset Jacob Rees-Mogg voted against equal gay rights nine times
2. **H.** Between 2001 – 2010, MP for Maidenhead Theresa May voted against Labour's anti-terrorism laws forty-nine times
3. **A.** Between 2002 – 2004, MP for Christchurch Christopher Chope voted against the hunting ban seven times.
4. **D.** Between 2012 – 2013, MP for Stone Bill Cash voted against slowing the rise in rail fares five times.
5. **C.** Between 2012 – 2015, MP for Lichfield Michael Fabricant voted against increasing the tax rate applied to income over £150,000 twelve times.
6. **B** Between 2008 – 2022, MP for Raleigh and Wickford Mark Francois voted against more EU integration one hundred and thirteen times.
7. **J.** Between 2010 – 2015, MP for Suffolk Coastal Thérèse Coffey voted against smoking bans four times.
8. **F.** Between 2011 – 2015, MP for Chingford and Woodford Green Iain Duncan Smith voted against bankers' bonus tax fourteen times.
9. **G.** Between 2013 – 2014, MP for South Northamptonshire Andrea Leadsom voted against greater regulation of gambling four times.
10. **I.** Between 2015 – 2022, MP for Uxbridge and South Ruislip Boris Johnson voted against higher taxes on banks eight times.

PAGES 10-11: MATCH THE QUOTE TO THE TORY

1. Boris Johnson (Telegraph – 5 August 2018)
2. Desmond Swayne (Telegraph – 17 July 2020)
3. Priti Patel (Home Affairs Committee – 2 February 2022)
4. Dominic Raab (PoliticsHome – 24 January 2011)
5. Michael Fabricant (Twitter – 18 May 2022)
6. Nadine Dorries (House of Commons – 5 February 2013)
7. Jacob Rees-Mogg (LBC Radio - 4 November 2019)
8. Lee Anderson (Twitter – 19 January 2023)
9. Christopher Chope (House of Commons – 17 January 2013)
10. Suella Braverman (House of Commons – 31 October 2022)

PAGES 12–13: TORIES BY NUMBERS: PANDEMIC EDITION

1. F – 37,000,000,000 = The two-year budget (in pounds) set by the government in 2020 for the NHS Test and Trace app.[75]
2. E. 50 = The percentage the government subsidised for food and non-alcoholic drinks during Rishi Sunak's Eat Out to Help Out scheme.[76]
3. A. 5 = Number of Cobra meetings about the developing Covid outbreak that Boris Johnson skipped, according to Michael Gove.[77]
4. D. 100,000 = The number of daily Covid tests that health secretary Matt Hancock was trying to hit by the end of April 2020 (it later emerged that he was concerned prioritising tests in care homes would hamper his efforts to hit his target).[78]
5. G. 4,000,000,000 = The value (in pounds) of PPE purchased by the government during the first year of the pandemic which was later burned after being found to be unusable.[79]
6. H. 47 = The number of companies that were awarded lucrative PPE contracts after referrals from government officials, in what became known as the 'VIP lane'.[80]
7. C. 2= Distance (in metres) that people from different households were required to maintain in order to comply with the government's social distancing rules.
8. B. 4,500,000,000 = Amount (in pounds) lost to Covid fraud that a government taskforce was set up to chase before being shut down in January 2023 by HMRC, which claimed that pursuing the money didn't provide the best value for the taxpayer.[81]
9. J. 300,034,974,000 = The number (or at least, something resembling a number) that Priti Patel used during a press conference on 11 April 2020 when talking about how many Covid tests had been carried out in the UK to that point.[82]
10. I. 39.1 = The percentage of A-level results that were downgraded in 2020 as a result of the algorithm spearheaded by then-education secretary Gavin Williamson.[83]

PAGE 14: FREE SCHOOL MEALS WORDSEARCH

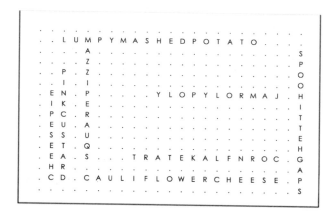

PAGES 16–18: TORY PUB QUIZ: ROUND ONE

1. B – South Africa
2. C – Jonathan Gullis
3. C – Get lost trying to exit the room
4. D – The under-occupancy penalty
5. A – Speeding
6. C – Nadine Dorries
7. C: He boycotted it due to players taking the knee
8. D – Alok Sharma
9. B – Minister for Brexit Opportunities and Government Efficiency
10. B – Michael Gove

PAGE 19: BARNARD CASTLE EYE TEST

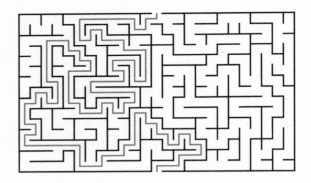

PAGE 20: NET ZERO (FUCKS GIVEN)

1. Going for a 30 min walk (0g CO2)
2. Making one Google search (0.2g CO2)
3. Using an eco-friendly lightbulb (18W) for 4 hours (30g CO2)
4. Boiling a kettle (50g CO2)
5. Eating one banana (70g CO2)
6. Eating one tomato (160g CO2)
7. Using a mobile phone for one hour (172g CO2)
8. Drinking a pint of beer (665g CO2)
9. Taking a hot shower for 10 minutes (2kg CO2)
10. Flying from London to New York in a commercial jet (900KG CO2)

PAGE 21: REAL OR FAKE TORY EXPENSES CLAIM?
REAL
1. Iain Duncan once claimed £39 for a single breakfast (despite previously claiming that he could comfortably live on just £53 a week).[84]
3. David Heathcote-Amory claimed £380 worth of horse manure.[85]
4. Former Tory MP Sir Peter Viggers claimed over £30,000 in gardening expenses, including a 'floating duck island' worth £1,645.[86]
6. Andrew Selous claimed 55p for a mug of Horlicks.[87]
8. Tory Peer Ed Vaizey claimed 8p for a 350-yard car journey.[88]
9. James Arbuthnot attempted to claim £43.56 for three garlic peelers.[89]

FAKE
2. Paul Beresford claimed two iPod Shuffles in the space of a week after leaving one on a train.
5. Michelle Donelan claimed fifteen scratch cards on expenses after including them in her lunchtime meal deals, but paid the money back after winning £1,000.
7. Chris Heaton-Harris claimed a variety of magazine subscriptions, including Total Guitar, Classic Rock, and The Beano.
10. Pauline Latham claimed £204 for four tickets to Mamma Mia! In London's West End

PAGES 22–23: HATE CRIME NATION
1. D – There were 4,355 recorded hate crimes against transgender people in England and Wales in 2022.
2. C – Greater Manchester was the police force area with the highest number of recorded hate crimes per 100,000 population, with 457 between 2021 and 2022.
3. C – Recorded hate crimes on people with disabilities in Scotland increased by 1,287 percent between 2010 and 2022, from 48 to 666.
4. A – Between 2016 and 2017, the number of racially motivated hate crimes recorded in England and Wales increased from 49,419 to 62,685.
5. B – The Covid-19 pandemic saw a 15 percent increase in the number of attacks on mosques.

PAGE 24: TORY MATHS
1. One hundred and twenty thousand units of PPE will be provided.
2. Boris is now walking west.
3. There are zero ferries.
4. Matt and Gina are standing five centimetres apart.
5. Three million, six hundred and ninety thousand people are now using a food bank.

PAGES 26–27: TORIES: A HISTORY

```
¹B
 L
 A                       ²G
 C                        R
 K              ³B  L  O  O  D
 W          ⁴D     ⁵Q         C
⁶E  D  W  I  N  A  C  U  R  R  I  E      R
 D              N     E               R
 N     ⁷W       G     S
 E      E       E     T
 S     ⁸S  C  A  R  G  I  L  L        I
 D      T                  O
 A      L            ⁹S  N  A  T  C  H  E  R
 Y      A                  S
        N
        D
```

PAGES 28–29: QUICKFIRE BREXIT ROUND

1. They were the three stooges of the apocalypse, aka the Brexit secretaries/
    secretaries of state for exiting the European Union. We had three between July
    2016 and January 2020 can you believe.
2. David Cameron inexplicably began singing to himself, despite having just
    announced his resignation.
3. The DUP.
4. The protocol which aimed to prevent an evident border was known as the Irish
    Backstop.
5. Article 50.
6. Michael Gove, Steve Baker, Priti Patel, Anne-Marie Trevelyan, and Douglas
    Carswell were/are all members of the European Research Group.
7. Several Leave campaigners made spurious claims about Turkey joining the EU.[90]
8. Boris Johnson described his Brexit deal as 'oven ready', although the fact that aspects
    of it were still being revisited three years later suggests that it probably wasn't.
9. Jacob Rees-Mogg co-founded Somerset Capital Management, which – in
    addition to setting up a hedge fund in Ireland – also warned prospective clients
    about the dangers of a hard Brexit, which Rees-Mogg was publicly pushing for.
10. The report accused the government of avoiding investigating whether Russia
    interfered with public opinion.

PAGE 30: NOTHING SAYS TORY BRITAIN LIKE … HOMELESS CHILDREN?

1. London (73,810 children living in temporary accommodation)
1. Birmingham (8,312)
2. Manchester (3,649)
3. Luton (1,851)
4. Brighton and Hove (1,360)

5. Milton Keynes (1,182)
6. Basildon (780)
7. Slough (521)
8. Harlow (328)
9. Hastings (314)

PAGE 31: LEAVING A TOWN NEAR YOU
Triangle: library
Square: youth club
Circle: park
Rectangle: playing field
Hexagon: community centre

PAGE 32: JOIN THE DOTS

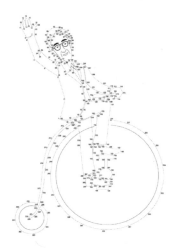

AGES 34–35: #TORYSCMU ANAGRAMS: ROUND ONE
1. Allegra Stratton
2. Crete
3. Cocaine
4. Turnips
5. Evgeny Lebedev
6. Grantham
7. Sunlit uplands
8. Marcus Rashford
9. Hands, Face, Space
10. Jennifer Arcuri

PAGES 36–37: HOW MUCH????

1. C. East Midlands – £246,092
2. E. South East – £394,543
3. I. Yorkshire and the Humber – £203,635
4. D. North East – £156,912
5. B. London – £523,325
6. H. West Midlands – £245,132
7. G. South West – £326,035
8. A. East of England – £351,898
9. F. North West – £211,759

PAGES 38–39: WHAT A LOAD OF AWFUL CUTS

SOUTH TYNESIDE
GATESHEAD

WIGAN
SALFORD
OLDHAM

CAMDEN
WESTMINSTER
HAMMERSMITH & FULHAM
KENSINGTON & CHELSEA

SLOUGH

PAGE 40: LOCKDOWN PARTY SHOPPING LIST

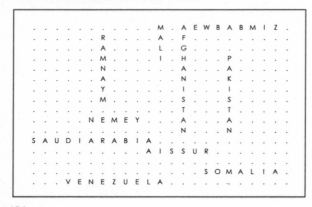

PAGE 41: DOMINIC RAAB'S GEOGRAPHY CHALLENGE

1. Iceland
2. Sweden
3. Germany
4. Portugal
5. Italy
6. Russia
7. Belarus
8. Ukraine
9. Romania
10. Turkey

PAGES 42-43: HOW TO LOSE A BILLION POUNDS IN SIX MONTHS

1. C – Tripoli
2. D – Muammar Gaddafi
3. B – Volcano
4. D – It was the only flag that was just one colour and had no design
5.

PAGE 47: KEEPING UP WITH THE SUNAKS

WEALTHIER THAN THE SUNAKS

— James Dyson (£23 billion)
— Mike Ashley (£3.84 billion)
— Alan Sugar (£1.074 billion)
— Paul McCartney and Nancy Shevell (£950 million)
— JK Rowling (£875 million)
— King Charles III (£600 million)

POORER THAN THE SUNAKS

— Daniel Levy (£500 million)
— Elton John (£450 million)
— Simon Cowell (£390 million)
— Ed Sheeran (£300 million)

PAGE 51: TO THE REFRIGERATOR!

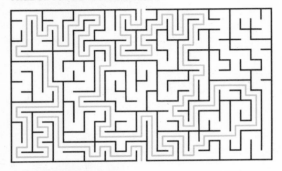

PAGE 53: FIND THE TORY

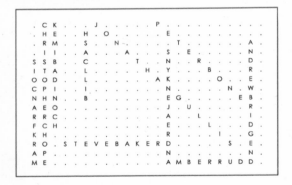

PAGE 55: THIS MIGHT HURT A LITTLE

Emily: lung
Brenda: eye
Kendal: kidney
Hassan: knee
Adanna: womb

PAGES 56–57: SPOT THE TORY STRONGHOLD
TORY STRONGHOLDS

— Raleigh and Wickford (31,000 majority)
— South Holland and the Deepings (30,838)
— Maldon (30,041)
— North East Cambridgeshire (29,993)
— Brentwood and Ongar (29,065)
— Louth and Horncastle (28,868)
— South Staffordshire (28,250)
— Castle Point (26,634)
— Boston and Skegness (25,621)
— Clacton (24,702)

LABOUR STRONGHOLDS

— Knowsley (39,942 majority)
— Bethnal Green and Bow (37,524)
— Liverpool, Riverside (37,043)
— Bootle (34,556)
— Hackney South and Shoreditch (33,985)
— Camberwell and Peckham (33,780)
— Hackney North and Stoke Newington (33,188)
— East Ham (33,176)
— Lewisham, Deptford (32,913)
— Garston and Halewood (31,624)

PAGE 58: JOIN THE DOTS

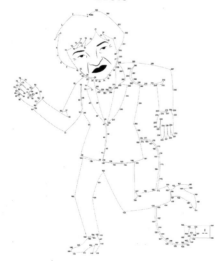

PAGES 59–61: TORY PUB QUIZ: ROUND TWO

1. A – Eat Out to Help Out
2. C – Lie down in front of bulldozers
3. C – The Holocaust
4. D – Saudi Arabia
5. B – Michelle Donelan
6. B – Food banks
7. D – Will Self
8. B – Ian Botham
9. D – Owen Paterson
10. C – Thursday

PAGES 64–65: I THINK WE SHOULD SEE OTHER CURRENCIES

1. G. Zloty – Poland
2. C. Rand – South Africa
3. H. Forint – Hungary
4. A. Yen – Japan
5. E. Dong – Vietnam
6. B. Lev – Bulgaria
7. F. Rial – Iran
8. J. Krona – Sweden
9. D. Baht – Thailand
10. I. Lek – Albania

PAGES 66–67: TORIES BY NUMBERS: PANDEMIC EDITION

1. D – 40 – New hospitals pledged by Boris Johnson in the 2019 Tories' 2019 election manifesto.[91]
2. H – 350,000,000 – Amount (in pounds) that the infamous 'Brexit bus' claimed that the UK sent to the EU every week.[92]
3. F – Percentage of the £320,000 fee for appearing on I'm a Celebrity... Get Me Out of Here! That Matt Hancock donated to charity.[93]
4. A – 126 – fixed penalty notices handed out by the Metropolitan Police during the so-called partygate scandal.[94]
5. G – 57 – the number of Lib Dem MPs who joined the coalition government in 2010.[95]
6. C – 44 – Length of time (in days) that Liz Truss spent as prime minister.[96]
7. E – The amount (in pounds) promised to the DUP over five years to help prop up Theresa May's minority government in 2018.[97]
8. I – 62 – Total number of resignations (ministers, private secretaries, trade envoys, and vice-chairmen) from Boris Johnson's government that forced his hand and led to his resignation in July 2022.[98]

9. B – 800,000 – Amount (in pounds) that former BBC chairman Richard Sharp helped to arrange for Boris Johnson.[99]
10. J – 253 – Distance (in miles) from 10 Downing Street to Barnard Castle.

PAGES 68–69: TORY TRUE OR FALSE: ROUND ONE
TRUE

1. In the run-up to the 2019 general election, Lee Anderson was caught on camera getting one of his friends to pretend to be an anti-Labour swing voter after forgetting that his microphone was still on.[100]
2. In 2022, Tory ex-minister John Redwood suggested that severe NHS bed shortages could be solved by simply adding more.[101]
5. In 2018 Tory backbencher Christopher Chope objected to a bill to make upskirting a criminal offence.[102]
7. While serving breakfast at a shelter in London shortly after becoming PM, Rishi Sunak asked a homeless man if he worked in business.[103]
8. Penny Mordaunt paid her way through sixth form by working as a magician's assistant.[104]

FALSE

3. In February 2011, Transport Secretary Justine Greening fell into the River Trent during the opening of a kayak club in Nottingham.
4. In 2017 a house owned by Jeremy Hunt was deemed 'unsuitable for human inhabitation' after a tenant was hospitalised with a severe lung infection.
6. Following the exit poll results at the 2019 general election, a Tory candidate in Hertfordshire rolled a cigarette using a £20 note.
9. A 2006 biography of Ted Heath claimed that the former PM once put an injured pigeon out of its misery by snapping its neck, but accidentally decapitated it in the process.
10. While on his honeymoon in 2014, Jonathan Gullis was taken to hospital after being bitten by a stray cat.

PAGE 70: HELP DAVID CAMERON FIND HIS SHED

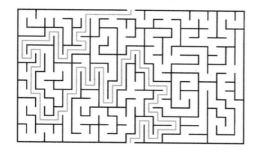

PAGE 73: FIND THE CHEESE!

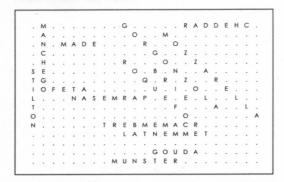

PAGES 74–75: TORIES: MASTERS OF THE LUCRATIVE SECOND JOB

1. F. Boris Johnson – £1,064,785
2. C. Nadine Dorries – £181,556
3. I. David Davis – £191,316
4. H. Chris Grayling – £224,487
5. D. Owen Paterson – £209,227
6. B. Geoffrey Cox – £2,191,387
7. J. Theresa May – £2,550,876
8. A. Fiona Bruce – £711,749
9. G. Sajid Javid – £361,566
10. E. John Redwood – £692,438

PAGES 76–77: THE LIZ TRUSSWORD

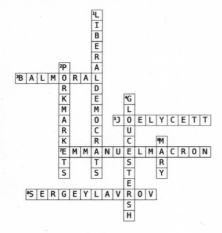

PAGES 78–79: GOOD MEMORIES

2010 Proposals to increase tuition fees result in student riots outside Conservative Party headquarters in London.

2011 Liam Fox resigns as defence secretary after letting a personal friend attend meetings that he wasn't cleared for.

2012 Andrew Mitchell resigns for an incident at Downing Street which would later become known as 'Plebgate'.

2013 Home Office deploys infamous 'go home' vans to areas of London with high immigrant populations.

2014 Culture secretary Maria Miller finally resigns after two years of intense scrutiny over her parliamentary expenses claims.

2015 A biography by Lord Ashcroft alleges that David Cameron took part in a peculiar initiation ceremony involving a pig and part of his anatomy.

2016 David Cameron announces EU referendum, which went famously well.

2017 Priti Patel resigns as international development secretary over unofficial meetings with Israelis.

2018 Amber Rudd resigns as home secretary, following strong criticism of her role in the treatment of Windrush generation migrants.

2019 The proroguing of Parliament, which was later ruled to be unlawful.

2020 Government puts Dido Harding in charge of NHS Test and Trace.

2021 Matt Hancock's caught-on-camera snog with Gina Coladangelo.

2022 Kwasi Kwarteng's disastrous 'mini budget' that almost wiped out the British economy.

2023 Nadhim Zahawi is sacked following an investigation into his tax affairs.

PAGE 80: JOIN THE DOTS

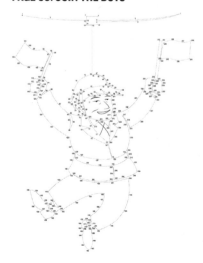

1. D. The Victorians: Twelve Titans Who Forged Britain – Jacob Rees-Mogg
2. E. The Angels of Lovely Lane – Nadine Dorries
3. J. Churchill: How One Man Made History – Boris Johnson
4. F. Snakes and Ladders: Navigating the Ups and Downs of Politics – Andrea Leadsom
5. C. The Abuse of Power – Theresa May
6. B. Ghosts of Empire: Britain's Legacies in the Modern World – Kwasi Kwarteng
7. I. The Path to Power – Margaret Thatcher
8. H. The Devil's Tune – Iain Duncan Smith
9. G. The Clematis Tree – Ann Widdecombe
10. A. Pandemic Diaries: The Inside Story of Britain's Battle Against Covid – Matt Hancock

PAGE 84: MEANINGLESS TORY SLOGANS

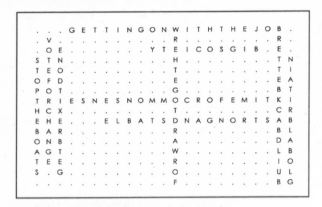

PAGES 86–87: TORY TRUE OR FALSE: ROUND TWO
TRUE

1. MP for Ashfield Lee Anderson claimed that would-be foodbank users could instead knock up nutritious meals for just thirty pence.[105]
5. In 2019, Foreign Office minister Mark Field was suspended after grabbing a female climate protester by the neck.[106]
8. During an episode of Good Evening Britain in 2018, Danny Dyer called former PM David Cameron a 'twat' during a discussion which included Jeremy Corbyn and Pamela Anderson.[107]
9. In 2017, Michael Fabricant appeared on Channel 4's First Dates.[108]
10. In 2018, Kemi Badenoch admitted that she once hacked Harriet Harman's official website, adding a fake blog post announcing that the Labour MP was backing Boris Johnson's bid to become London mayor.[109]

FALSE

2. In 2016, police were called to Bournemouth Beach after Jacob Rees-Mogg used a fake £20 note to hire a deckchair.
3. Gavin Williamson was so scared of veteran Labour MP Denis Skinner that he once hid in a toilet cubicle for almost twenty minutes to avoid running into him.
4. In 1996, Ken Clarke was removed from a plane by Turkish police after being caught smoking a cigar in the toilet.
6. In order to skip the queue at his local B&Q during the Covid pandemic, Tory backbencher Simon Fell told staff that he was there to make sure all safety procedures were being followed, before buying three tins of paint and a patio heater.
7. In 2011, Minister for Sport Hugh Robertson choked on an egg sandwich while showing VIPs around the London Olympic stadium, and was given the Heimlich manoeuvre by Lennox Lewis.

PAGES 88–89: THE PRETENTIOUS BLUSTER OF BORIS JOHNSON

1. B. Gibbering rictus[110] – Term used to describe someone who is open-mouthed with fear
2. G. Hogwhimpering[111] – Adjective for extreme drunkenness
3. H. Maenads[112] – The female followers of the Greek god of wine, Dionysus. Known for their drunken behaviour
4. E. Poule de luxe[113] – French slang for an expensive prostitute
5. C. Hypothalamus[114] – The part of the brain that stimulates sex drive
6. I. Ziggurats[115] – An ancient Mesopotamian temple
7. D. Boondoggle[116] – A wasteful, fraudulent, or unnecessary project
8. J. Hottentot[117] – Seventeenth-century racial term to describe nomadic South African pastoralists
9. A. Swankpot[118] – Antiquated term for a conceited person
10. F. Popinjay[119] – Archaic term for a parrot. Can be used to describe a talkative person

PAGES 92–93: BRITANNIA UNHINGED

1. B - Once they enter the workplace, the British are among the worst idlers in the world. We work among the lowest hours, we retire early and our productivity is poor.[120]
2. D - But why would a student put themselves through the hard graft when the jobs are open to those who have managed to spend their university days in the pub as well as the library?[121]
3. A - We must stop bailing out the reckless, avoiding all risk, and rewarding laziness.[122]
4. C - If indifferent parenting and mediocre schooling have contributed to an erosion of the British work ethic, some argue it has been further exacerbated by an increasingly pervasive celebrity culture.[123]
5. B - Instead, attracted by the idea of longer lie-ins for future generations some in Britain want their children to sit back and enjoy the fruits of their prosperity.[124]

PAGES 94–95: WHO AM I?

1. Gavin Williamson (or, rather, Sir Gavin Williamson)
2. Nadine Dorries
3. John Bercow
4. Priti Patel
5. Matt Hancock

PAGE 96: JOIN THE DOTS

PAGE 97: QUESTIONABLE ARMS EXPORTS

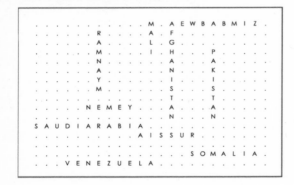

PAGES 100–101: PARTY OR NO PARTY?
NOT A PARTY

1. You're alone in a room with Rishi Sunak. He is sitting three metres away and offering his thoughts on the Bank of England's latest inflation statement.
3. You are sitting alone in the Downing Street garden, reflecting on the terrible loss of life caused by the Covid pandemic.

5. A colleague emails to ask if their department can have a small drinks reception after work. You decline the request as it's important to set a good example while lockdown rules are in place.

7. During a visit to a local hospital, you pay tribute to the hard work of staff, and reassure them that their wellbeing is at the forefront of your mind. You are wearing a mask and maintaining a safe distance at all times.

9. It's been a long week and you want to let your hair down. You crack open a bottle of wine and settle down to watch television with members of your own household.

PARTY

2. You are second from the back in a forty-six-man conga line. The person behind you throws up and a chunk of carrot lands your shoe.

4. Michael Gove has his arse well and truly wedged in the photocopier. You and sixteen other people gather round and laugh at him until the fire brigade arrives.

6. Dominic Cummings is doing the funky chicken on your desk and encouraging people to drink vodka from a shoe. Somebody throws a takeaway pizza like a frisbee and it hits a ceiling fan, showering everyone in ham and pineapple.

8. An extremely flustered Matt Hancock emerges from the Downing Street broom cupboard and gives you a high five. He is not wearing any trousers and you can't help but notice that his hand is quite sticky.

10. Karaoke is in full swing and the crowd is going wild for Rishi Sunak's rousing rendition of Bohemian Rhapsody. You take a quick break from shaving off a junior minister's eyebrows to piss through an open window. Larry the Cat – sitting directly below – is not best pleased.

N.B. we don't know that any of the above actually happened – these are just jokes, don't sue us.

PAGES 102–103: VICTORIAN SHOPPING WITH JACOB REES-MOGG

1. J. Snuff – Tobacconist
2. H Clove rocks – Confectioner
3. F. Camphorated tincture of opium – Apothecary
4. B. A silk bonnet – Milliner
5. C. Pattern 1861 Enfield musketoon – Gunsmith
6. D. Cloth – Draper
7. G. A tankard of mead – Public house
8. I. Half a bushel of milk – Dairyman
9. E. A shoulder of mutton – Butcher
10. A. Four buttons and a packet of hair pins – Haberdashery

PAGE 104: A NUMBER TWO IN NUMBER TEN

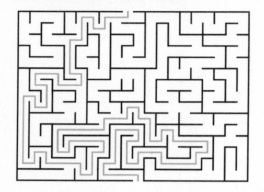

PAGE 105: TALLER OR SHORTER THAN RISHI SUNAK?
TALLER THAN RISHI SUNAK
— Ten cans of Pringles (seven feet, five inches)
— Two hundred Maltesers (six feet, six inches)
— The Venus de Milo (six feet, seven inches)
— Three Fender Stratocaster guitars (six feet, four inches)
— An Olympic spec men's javelin (eight feet, five inches)
— The Mars Curiosity Rover (seven feet, two inches)

SHORTER THAN RISHI SUNAK
— 2022 Nissan Micra (four feet, eight inches)
— Mother Teresa (five feet, zero inches)
— The Mona Lisa (two feet, five inches)
— Forty Big Macs (four feet, seven inches)

PAGES 106–107: #TORYSCMU: ANAGRAMS ROUND TWO
1. Windsor Framework
2. Lettuce
3. Greensill Capital
4. Michael Fallon
5. Jimmy Savile
6. Hostile environment policy
7. Steve Baker
8. Fields of wheat
9. Sebastian Fox
10. Joe Lycett

PAGE 108: TORY CHANCELLORS CROSSWORD

Crossword solution grid:

Across:
- 3. JEREMY HUNT
- 5. SAJID JAVID
- 6. GEORGE OSBORNE

Down:
- 1. JOHN MAJOR
- 2. KEN CLARKE
- 4. RISHI SUNAK
- 5. KWASI KWARTENG
- 7. NORMAN LAMONT
- 8. PHILIP HAMMOND
- 9. NADHIM ZAHAWI

PAGES 110–113: GUESS THE TORY FROM THE CHILD'S DRAWING

1. John Major
2. Margaret Thatcher
3. Jonathan Gullis
4. Jacob Rees-Mogg

PAGES 114–116: TORY PUB QUIZ: ROUND THREE

1. C – Northern Ireland
2. B – Leeds
3. D – Universal Credit
4. B – Suella Braverman
5. B – Jeremy Hunt
6. C: Nobody has ever committed a crime after being executed
7. C – Woke culture
8. A – Michelle Mone
9. B – He once strangled a dog to death
10. D – Johnny Mercer

REFERENCES

p.8: AWFUL TORY VOTING RECORDS
1. www.theyworkforyou.com (accessed 10/07/2023).

p.12: TORIES BY NUMBERS: PANDEMIC EDITION
2. www.worldometers.info/coronavirus/ (accessed 10/07/2023).

p.14: FREE SCHOOL MEALS WORDSEARCH
3. www.theyworkforyou.com/divisions/pw-2020-10-21-154-commons (accessed 10/07/2023).

p.20: NET ZERO
4. Michael Savage, 'Cameron's decision to cut 'green crap' now costs each household in England £150 a year', www.theguardian.com/money/2022/mar/19/david-cameron-green-crap-energy-prices (accessed 10/07/2023).
5. Fiona Harvey, 'UK government scraps green homes grant after six months', www.theguardian.com/environment/2021/mar/27/uk-government-scraps-green-homes-grant-after-six-months (accessed 10/07/2023).
6. Faye Brown, 'Ban on fracking to be lifted as part of Liz Truss's energy plan', www.news.sky.com/story/ban-on-fracking-to-be-lifted-as-part-of-liz-trusss-energy-plan-12692646 (accessed 10/07/2023).
7. Lizzy Buchan, 'Rishi Sunak racked up £38,500 bill flying by private jet to Tory events', www.mirror.co.uk/news/politics/rishi-sunak-racked-up-38500-30133334 (accessed 10/07/2023).

8. www.clevercarbon.io/carbon-footprint-of-common-items (accessed 10/07/2023).

p.22: HATE CRIME NATION
9. 'Hate Crime Statistics', www.commonslibrary.parliament.uk/research-briefings/cbp-8537/ (accessed 10/07/2023).

p.27: TORIES: A HISTORY
10. Michael Savage, '"A historic wrong": Government set to announce compensation for victims of contaminated blood scandal', www.theguardian.com/society/2022/aug/06/a-historic-wrong-government-set-to-announce-compensation-for-victims-of-contaminated-blood-scandal (accessed 24/07/2023).
11. Rowena Mason, 'Edwina Currie voices regrets over Jimmy Savile inquiry criticism', www.theguardian.com/media/2014/jun/26/edwina-currie-regret-jimmy-savile-broadmoor (accessed 10/07/2023).
12. '1971: Councils defy Thatcher milk ban', www.news.bbc.co.uk/onthisday/hi/dates/stories/june/15/newsid_4486000/4486571.stm (accessed 10/07/2023).

p.29: QUICKFIRE BREXIT ROUND
13. Boris Johnson, 'A deal is oven-ready. Let's get Brexit done and take this country forward', www.telegraph.co.uk/politics/2019/11/05/deal-oven-ready-get-brexit-done-take-country-forward/ (accessed 24/07/2023).
14. Dan Sabbagh, Luke Harding, and Andrew Roth, 'Russia report reveals UK government failed to investigate Kremlin interference', www.theguardian.com/world/2020/jul/21/russia-report-reveals-uk-government-failed-to-address-kremlin-interference-scottish-referendum-brexit (accessed 24/07/2023).

p.30: NOTHING SAYS TORY BRITAIN LIKE... HOMELESS CHILDREN?
15. 'At least 271,000 people are homeless in England today', www.england.shelter.org.uk/media/press_release/at_least_271000_people_are_homeless_in_england_today (accessed 10/07/2023).
16. Ruby Lott-Lavigna, 'The Tories pledged to end rough sleeping by 2024. Will they?', www.opendemocracy.net/en/rough-sleeping-conservative-manifesto-pledge-bob-blackman-homelessness/ (accessed 10/07/2023).

p.31: LEAVING A TOWN NEAR YOU
17. Gareth Davies, Charles Boutaud, Hazel Sheffield and Emma Youle, 'Revealed: The thousands of public spaces lost to the council funding crisis', www.thebureauinvestigates.com/stories/2019-03-04/sold-from-under-you (accessed 24/07/2023).

p.34: #TORYSCMU: ANAGRAMS ROUND ONE
18. Mattha Busby and Damien Gayle, 'Michael Gove admits to taking cocaine on "several occasions"', www.theguardian.com/politics/2019/jun/07/michael-gove-admits-to-taking-cocaine-on-several-social-occasions (accessed 24/07/2023).

19. 'Boris Johnson was warned of Lebedev security concerns, says Cummings', www.bbc.co.uk/news/uk-politics-60765665 (accessed 24/07/2023).

p.35: #TORYSCMU: ANAGRAMS ROUND ONE

20. Neil Sears, Sam Greenhill and Guy Adams, 'Boris Johnson only came round to mine for technology lessons, says ex-model who received thousands in public money', www.dailymail.co.uk/news/article-7500453/Ex-model-said-Boris-Johnson-came-round-technology-lessons.html (accessed 24/07/2023).

p.36: HOW MUCH????

21. 'John Healey responds to the English Housing Survey' www.labour.org.uk/press/john-healey-responds-to-the-english-housing-survey/ (accessed 10/07/2023).

22. May Bulman, 'Government has failed to build a single 'starter home' after promising 200,000, watchdog finds', www.independent.co.uk/news/uk/home-news/starter-homes-housing-first-time-buyers-national-audit-office-report-a9185371.html (accessed 10/07/2023).

p.38: WHAT A LOAD OF AWFUL CUTS

23. Felicity Lawrence, Niamh McIntyre and Patrick Butler, 'Labour councils in England hit harder by austerity than Tory areas', www.theguardian.com/business/2020/jun/21/exclusive-labour-councils-in-england-hit-harder-by-austerity-than-tory-areas (accessed 24/07/2023).

24. Cahal Milmo, 'Council cuts due to austerity 'twice as deep' in England as rest of Britain, study', www.inews.co.uk/news/uk/council-cuts-due-to-austerity-twice-as-deep-in-england-as-rest-of-britain-study-206530#:~:text=Among%20the%20ten%20worst%20affected%20English%20councils%20were,in%20Wales%20in%20was%2023%20per%20cent%20%28Denbighshire%29 (accessed 24/07/2023).

p.41: DOMINIC RAAB'S GEOGRAPHY CHALLENGE

25. Jack Beresford, 'UK Foreign Secretary Dominic Raab doesn't know the difference between the Irish Sea and Red Sea', www.irishpost.com/news/dominic-raab-irish-sea-169391 (accessed 10/07/2023).

26. 'Dominic Raab under fire over Dover-Calais comments', www.bbc.co.uk/news/uk-politics-46142188 (accessed 10/07/2023).

p.50: PARTY GAME: EARN A TORY PEERAGE

27. Jon Stone, 'Tories gave donors seats in House of Lords after they donated millions to party, investigation finds', www.independent.co.uk/news/uk/politics/tory-donors-house-lords-peers-theresa-may-boris-johnson-labour-a9231061.html (accessed 24/07/2023).

p.55: THIS MIGHT HURT A LITTLE

28. www.commonslibrary.parliament.uk/research-briefings/cbp-7281/#:~:text=The%20waiting%20list%20for%20hospital%20treatment%20rose%20to,treatment%20target%20has%20not%20been%20met%20since%202016 (accessed 24/07/2023).

p.56: SPOT THE TORY STRONGHOLD

29. 'General Election 2019: Marginality', www.commonslibrary.parliament.uk/general-election-2019-marginality/ (accessed 10/07/2023).

p.59: TORY PUB QUIZ: ROUND TWO

30. Dan Bloom, 'Squirming Boris Johnson repeats promise to lie in front of Heathrow bulldozers', www.mirror.co.uk/news/uk-news/squirming-boris-johnson-repeats-promise-21056766 (accessed 10/07/2023).

31. Tim Baker, 'Andrew Bridgen: MP kicked out of Tory party after comparing COVID vaccines to Holocaust', news.sky.com/story/andrew-bridgen-mp-kicked-out-of-tory-party-after-comparing-covid-vaccines-to-holocaust-12866848 (accessed 10/07/2023).

p.60: TORY PUB QUIZ: ROUND TWO

32. Matt Broomfield, 'UK arms sales to Saudi Arabia 'worth £5.6bn under David Cameron', www.independent.co.uk/news/uk/politics/uk-has-sold-ps5-6bn-of-military-hardware-to-saudi-arabia-under-david-cameron-research-reveals-a6797861.html (accessed 10/07/2023).

33. Nicholas Watt, 'Bishops blame David Cameron for food bank crisis', www.theguardian.com/politics/2014/feb/20/bishops-blame-cameron-food-bank-crisis (accessed 10/07/2023).

34. BBC, 'Politics Live', www.bbc.co.uk/programmes/p072z3yr (accessed 25/07/2023).

p.64: I THINK WE SHOULD SEE OTHER CURRENCIES

35. Michel Santi, '16 September 1992: The Black Wednesday That Changed Britain's Fate', www.luxuo.com/homepage-slider/16-september-1992-the-black-wednesday-that-changed-britains-fate.html (accessed 10/07/2023).

36. Graeme Wearden, 'Pound hits all-time low against dollar

after mini-budget rocks markets', www.theguardian.com/business/2022/sep/25/city-braces-for-more-volatility-mini-budget-rocks-pound-parity-dollar-bond-tax (accessed 10/07/2023).
37. 'How has Brexit affected the value of sterling?', www.economicsobservatory.com/how-has-brexit-affected-the-value-of-sterling (accessed 10/07/2023).

p.73: FIND THE CHEESE!
38. Liam James, 'Liz Truss's biggest gaffes and awkward moments', www.independent.co.uk/news/uk/politics/liz-truss-cheese-speech-gaffes-awkward-b2207586.html (accessed 24/07/2023).

p.74: TORIES: MASTERS OF THE LUCRATIVE SECOND JOB
39. Basit Mahmood, 'Tory MPs rake in £15.2 million from second jobs while telling striking workers to show pay restraint', www.leftfootforward.org/2023/01/tory-mps-rake-in-15-2-million-from-second-jobs-while-telling-striking-workers-to-show-pay-restraint/ (accessed 10/07/2023).

p.78: GOOD MEMORIES
40. 'Priti Patel quits cabinet over Israel meetings row', www.bbc.co.uk/news/uk-politics-41923007 (accessed 10/07/2023).
41. Richard Partington, Aubrey Allegretti, 'Kwasi Kwarteng's mini budget: key points at a glance', www.theguardian.com/uk-news/2022/sep/23/kwasi-kwarteng-mini-budget-key-points-at-a-glance (accessed 10/07/2023).
42. 'Liam Fox quits as defence secretary', www.bbc.co.uk/news/uk-politics-15300751 (accessed 10/07/2023).

43. 'Amber Rudd resigns as home secretary', www.bbc.co.uk/news/uk-politics-43944988 (accessed 10/07/2023).
44. Peter Walker, 'Andrew Mitchell and the Plebgate affair explained for non-Brits', www.theguardian.com/politics/2014/nov/27/plebgate-andrew-mitchell-explain-non-brits (accessed 10/07/2023).
45. 'New chair of coronavirus 'test and trace' programme appointed', www.gov.uk/government/news/new-chair-of-coronavirus-test-and-trace-programme-appointed (accessed 10/07/2023).
46. Rowena Mason, 'David Cameron publicly denies Lord Ashcroft pig allegation for first time', www.theguardian.com/politics/2015/sep/27/david-cameron-denies-lord-ashcroft-allegations-call-me-dave-dead-pig (accessed 10/07/2023).

p.79: GOOD MEMORIES
47. Sophie Morris, 'Nadhim Zahawi sacked as Tory chairman over tax affairs row', www.news.sky.com/story/nadhim-zahawi-sacked-as-tory-chairman-over-tax-affairs-row-12793431 (accessed 10/07/2023).
48. Jessica Elgot, 'What is prorogation and why is Boris Johnson using it?', www.theguardian.com/politics/2019/aug/28/what-is-prorogation-prorogue-parliament-boris-johnson-brexit (accessed 10/07/2023).
49. Rob Pattinson, Tom Wells, 'MATT'S AWKWARD! Watch Matt Hancock affair video as he kisses Gina Coladangelo in his office after checking the coast is clear', www.thesun.co.uk/news/15397207/watch-matt-hancock-video-health-secretary-kissing-gina-coladangelo/ (accessed 10/07/2023).

50. 'Maria Miller quits as culture secretary after expenses row', www.bbc.co.uk/news/uk-politics-26951464, (accessed 10/07/2023).
51. Paul Lewis, Jeevan Vasagar, Rachel Williams, Matthew Taylor, 'Student protest over fees turns violent', www.theguardian.com/education/2010/nov/10/student-protest-fees-violent (accessed 10/07/2023).
52. Patrick Wintour, 'Go home' vans to be scrapped after experiment deemed a failure', www.theguardian.com/uk-news/2013/oct/22/go-home-vans-scrapped-failure (accessed 10/07/2023).
53. Kate Day, 'David Cameron announces EU referendum on June 23', www.politico.eu/article/david-cameron-announces-eu-referendum-on-june-23-brexit-deal/ (accessed 10/07/2023).

p.94: WHO AM I?
54. Sophie Morris, 'John Bercow: Former Speaker administratively suspended from Labour after bullying inquiry finds him guilty and bans him from parliament', www.news.sky.com/story/john-bercow-former-speaker-administratively-suspended-from-labour-after-bullying-inquiry-finds-him-guilty-and-bans-him-from-parliament-12560710 (accessed 10/07/2023).

p.95: WHO AM I?
55. Tom Peck, 'Priti Patel was smirking double hard as she tried to style out the government's most recent outrage', www.independent.co.uk/voices/priti-patel-rwanda-flight-immigration-pmqs-b2101944.html (accessed 10/07/2023).
56. 'Matt Hancock bids 'fond farewell' to his app after five years', www.bbc.co.uk/

news/technology-64162109 (accessed 10/07/2023).

p.97: QUESTIONABLE ARMS EXPORTS

57. Mark Townsend, '£17bn of UK arms sold to rights' abusers', www.theguardian.com/world/2021/jun/27/17bn-of-uk-arms-sold-to-rights-abusers (accessed 10/07/2023).

p.106: #TORYSCMU: ANAGRAMS ROUND TWO

58. 'David Cameron to be investigated by lobbying body', www.bbc.co.uk/news/uk-politics-56521708 (accessed 24/07/2023).

59. Heather Stewart and Rowena Mason, 'Michael Fallon quits as defence secretary, saying his behavious has "fallen short"', www.theguardian.com/politics/2017/nov/01/michael-fallon-quits-as-defence-secretary (accessed 24/07/2023).

60. 'No evidence for Boris Johnson's claim about Keir Starmer and Jimmy Savile', www.bbc.co.uk/news/60213975 (accessed 23/07/2023).

p.107: #TORYSCMU: ANAGRAMS ROUND TWO

61. James Kirkup and Robert Winnett, 'Theresa May interview: "We're going to give illegal migrants a really hostile reception"', www.telegraph.co.uk/news/uknews/immigration/9291483/Theresa-May-interview-Were-going-to-give-illegal-migrants-a-really-hostile-reception.html (accessed 24/07/2023).

62. Greg Evans, 'Tory MP Steve Baker roasted after referring to himself as 'Brexit hard man' on live TV', www.indy100.com/news/brexit-steve-baker-hard-man-erg-sky-news-twitter-response-8850871 (accessed 24/07/2023).

63. Randeep Ramesh Alice Ross, Rowena Mason and David Pegg, 'Grant Shapps did not publish own name on marketing website, analysis finds', www.theguardian.com/politics/2015/mar/25/grant-shapps-did-not-publish-own-name-on-marketing-website-analysis-finds (accessed 24/07/2023).

64. Jacob Solworthy, 'Joe Lycett hailed as 'genius' after appearing on BBC politics show as 'right-wing' Tory supporter', www.independent.co.uk/arts-entertainment/tv/news/joe-lycett-bbc-liz-truss-b2159376.html (accessed 25/07/2023).

p.114: TORY PUB QUIZ: ROUND THREE

65. Robyn Vinter, Rowena Mason, 'Health and wealth divides in UK worsening despite 'leveling up' drive, report finds', www.theguardian.com/inequality/2022/dec/04/health-and-wealth-divides-in-uk-worsening-despite-levelling-up-drive-report-finds (accessed 10/07/2023).

66. 'HS2 cost passes £40bn, with £1bn to be spent before a vote takes place', www.stophs2.org/news/8268-hs2-cost-passes-40bn-with-1bn-to-be-spent-before-a-vote-takes-place (accessed 10/07/2023).

67. 'Universal Credit and food banks', www.trusselltrust.org/what-we-do/research-advocacy/universal-credit-and-foodbank-use/ (accessed 10/07/2023).

p.115: TORY PUB QUIZ: ROUND THREE

68. 'PM and Home Secretary attacks on lawyers betray a startling ignorance', www.barcouncil.org.uk/resource/pm-and-home-secretary-attacks-on-lawyers-betray-a-startling-ignorance.html (accessed 10/07/2023).

69. Helier Cheung, 'Why Jeremy Hunt's 'Japanese' wife gaffe is a bad mistake', www.bbc.co.uk/news/world-asia-china-45004765 (accessed 10/07/2023).

70. Faye Brown, 'Lee Anderson: New Tory deputy chairman says he would support return of death penalty', www.news.sky.com/story/lee-anderson-new-tory-deputy-chairman-says-he-would-support-return-of-death-penalty (accessed 10/07/2023).

71. Stephen Bush, 'Truss blames 'woke culture' for failings. Is anyone listening?', www.ft.com/content/c1c0a3c8-f811-4ad9-bce1-97f422436a1a (accessed 10/07/2023).

p.116: TORY PUB QUIZ: ROUND THREE

72. Peter Davidson, 'Michelle Mone to take 'leave of absence' from House of Lords amid PPE allegations', www.dailyrecord.co.uk/news/politics/michelle-mone-take-leave-absence-28665268 (accessed 10/07/2023).

73. Maya Oppenheim, 'Michael Heseltine admits to strangling his mother's dog to death: "If you have a dog that turns, you just cannot risk it"', www.independent.co.uk/news/people/michael-heseltine-mother-dog-strangled-to-death-a7390781.html (accessed 10/07/2023).

74. Erin Black, 'What is the suddenly famous 'Plymouth Herald comments section'?', www.plymouthherald.co.uk/news/plymouth-news/what-plymouth-herald-comments-section-2128630 (accessed 10/07/2023).

p.119: ANSWERS: TORIES BY NUMBERS: PANDEMIC EDITION

75. www.fullfact.org/health/test-and-trace-37-billion/ (accessed 10/07/2023).

76. www.gov.uk/guidance/get-a-discount-with-the-eat-out-to-help-out-scheme (accessed 10/07/2023).

77. Peter Walker, 'Boris Johnson missed five coronavirus Cobra meetings, Michael Gove says', www.theguardian.com/world/2020/apr/19/michael-gove-fails-to-deny-pm-missed-five-coronavirus-cobra-meetings (accessed 10/07/2023).

78. 'I want to hit my target, Matt Hancock said as he called in a favour from George Osborne', www.telegraph.co.uk/news/2023/02/28/how-matt-hancock-achieved-100k-daily-covid-test-target/ (accessed 10/07/2023).

79. '£4 billion of unusable PPE bought in first year of pandemic will be burnt to "to generate power"', www.committees.parliament.uk/committee/127/public-accounts-committee/news/171306/4-billion-of-unusable-ppe-bought-in-first-year-of-pandemic-will-be-burnt-to-generate-power/ (accessed 10/07/2023).

80. Helen Collis, 'High Court finds UK's VIP lane for PPE contracts 'unlawful', www.politico.eu/article/high-court-uk-vip-lane-ppe-contract-unlawful/ (accessed 10/07/2023).

81. Charlotte Gifford, 'Taskforce set up to chase £4.5bn Covid fraud not worth the money, says HMRC', www.telegraph.co.uk/money/consumer-affairs/covid-fraud-fighting-team-not-worth-money-says-hmrc/ (accessed 10/07/2023).

82. Hannah Carmichael, 'Backlash as Priti Patel gives wrong number of coronavirus tests', www.thenational.scot/news/18375469.backlash-priti-patel-gives-wrong-number-coronavirus-tests/ (accessed 10/07/2023).

83. Richard Adams, Sally Weale, Caelainn Barr, 'A-level results: almost 40% of teacher assessments in England downgraded', www.theguardian.com/education/2020/aug/13/almost-40-of-english-students-have-a-level-results-downgraded (accessed 10/07/2023).

p.121: ANSWERS: REAL OR FAKE TORY EXPENSES CLAIM?

84. Jason Beattie, 'EXCLUSIVE: Iain Duncan Smith claimed £39 breakfast on expenses (that'd leave him £14 for the rest of the week)', www.mirror.co.uk/news/uk-news/iain-duncan-smith-claimed-breakfast-1810086 (accessed 10/07/2023).

85. 'MPs EXPENSES: How David Heathcoat-Amory spent £380 on 550 bags of horse manure (and £1.95 on sunflower seeds)', www.dailymail.co.uk/news/article-1180700/MPs-EXPENSES-How-David-Heathcoat-Amory-spent-380-550-bags-horse-manure-1-95-sunflower-seeds.html (accessed 10/07/2023).

86. 'Humiliated' Tory MP Peter Viggers quits over duck island expense claim', www.theguardian.com/politics/2009/may/23/mps-expenses-conservatives (accessed 10/07/2023).

87. 'MPs' expenses: the most bizarre claims', www.telegraph.co.uk/news/newstopics/mps-expenses/mps-expenses-in-pictures/6790519/MPs-expenses-the-most-bizarre-claims.html (accessed 10/07/2023).

88. 'MP claimed 8p for car journey', www.oxfordmail.co.uk/news/9346292.mp-claimed-8p-car-journey/ (accessed 10/07/2023).

89. 'More expenses embarrassment for MPs', www.dailystar.co.uk/news/more-expenses-embarrassment-for-mps-18039644 (accessed 10/07/2023).

p.122: ANSWERS: QUICKFIRE BREXIT ROUND

90. 'Austerity hitting Labour councils harder than Tory areas', www.governmentbusiness.co.uk/news/22062020/austerity-hitting-labour-councils-harder-tory-areas (accessed 10/07/2023).

p.128: ANSWERS: TORIES BY NUMBERS

91. 'PM confirms £3.7 billion for 40 hospitals in biggest hospital building programme in a generation', www.gov.uk/government/news/pm-confirms-37-billion-for-40-hospitals-in-biggest-hospital-building-programme-in-a-generation (accessed 10/07/2023).

92. Emer O'Toole, 'Boris Johnson says £350m Brexit bus figure was an 'underestimation', www.thenational.scot/news/19426977.boris-johnson-says-350m-brexit-bus-figure-underestimation/ (accessed 10/07/2023).

93. Alix Cuthbertson, 'Matt Hancock donates £10,000 of his £320,000 I'm a Celeb fee to two charities', news.sky.com/story/matt-hancock-donates-10-000-of-his-320-000-im-a-celeb-fee-to-two-charities-12796936 (accessed 10/07/2023).

94. Lizzie Dearden, 'Partygate investigation ends with 126 fines issued for at least eight events, Met Police say', www.independent.co.uk/news/

uk/politics/partygate-latest-met-police-fines-how-many-b2082611.html (accessed 10/07/2023).

95. David Cutts, Andrew Russell, 'From Coalition to Catastrophe: The Electoral Meltdown of the Liberal Democrats' academic. oup.com/pa/article/68/suppl_1/70/1403259 (accessed 10/07/2023).

96. George Parker, Sebastian Payne, Laura Hughes, 'The inside story of Liz Truss's disastrous 44 days in office', www.ft.com/content/736a695d-61f6-4e84-a567-fb92ed2a3dca (accessed 10/07/2023).

97. 'Confidence and Supply: Northern Ireland's £1 billion', www.commonslibrary. parliament.uk/confidence-and-supply-northern-irelands-1-billion/ (accessed 10/07/2023).

98. Robert Walker, 'Boris Johnson: the moral case for government resignations in July 2022', www.ncbi. nlm.nih.gov/pmc/articles/PMC9702785/, (accessed 10/07/2023).

99. Andrew McDonald, 'BBC Chairman Richard Sharp quits over report into Boris Johnson loan', www.politico.eu/article/bbc-chairman-richard-sharp-quit-report-boris-johnson-loan/ (accessed 10/07/2023).

p.129: ANSWERS: TORY TRUE OR FALSE: ROUND ONE
100. Jon Stone, 'Tory MP candidate caught getting friend to pose as anti-Labour swing voter, as party's disinformation campaign continues', www. independent.co.uk/news/uk/politics/general-election-latest-tory-fake-swing-voter-boris-johnson-crick-ashfield-lee-anderson-a9216986.html (accessed 10/07/2023).

101. www.twitter. com/johnredwood/status/1604004431405760512 (accessed 10/07/2023).

102. Peter Walker, 'Tory MP Christopher Chope blocks progress of upskirting bill', www.theguardian.com/world/2018/jun/15/tory-mp-christopher-chope-blocks-progress-of-upskirting-bill (accessed 10/07/2023).

103. Sophie Morris, 'Labour brand Rishi Sunak's shelter visit 'excruciating' after PM asks homeless man if he works in business', www.news.sky. com/story/labour-brand-rishi-sunaks-shelter-visit-excruciating-after-pm-asks-homeless-man-if-he-works-in-business-12774156 (accessed 10/07/2023).

104. Clive Hammond, 'Penny Mordaunt's colourful past as a magician's assistant', www.express.co.uk/news/uk/1636798/penny-mordaunt-news-boris-johnson-resignation-next-prime-minister-2022-election-spt, (accessed 10/07/2023).

p.132: ANSWERS: TORY TRUE OR FALSE: ROUND TWO
105. Karen Antcliff, 'Top chef says MP Lee Anderson talking nonsense as he shows what 30p meal looks like', www. nottinghampost.com/whats-on/food-drink/top-chef-says-mp-lee-7095205 (accessed 10/07/2023).

106. 'MP Mark Field accused of assaulting Greenpeace activist', www.bbc.co.uk/news/uk-48714864 (accessed 10/07/2023).

107. 'Danny Dyer Takes Down David Cameron In Hilarious TV Rant', www.lbc.co.uk/hot-topics/brexit/danny-dyer-takes-down-david-cameron-on-tv/ (accessed 10/07/2023).

108. Joe Mellor, 'Watch: Michael Fabricant's

appearance on First Dates is doing the rounds again', www.thelondoneconomic. com/news/watch-michael-fabricants-appearance-on-first-dates-is-doing-the-rounds-again-331747/ (accessed 10/07/2023).

109. Alex Hern, 'Bafflement over Tory MP's admission she hacked Harriet Harman's website', www.theguardian. com/technology/2018/apr/09/bafflement-over-tory-mps-admission-she-hacked-harriet-harmans-website (accessed 10/07/2023).

p.133: ANSWERS: THE PRETENTIOUS BLUSTER OF BORIS JOHNSON
110. Simon Walters, 'The mutton-headed old mugwump ker-splonked! Boris Johnson's colourful collection of insults for Jeremy Corbyn make a delicious epitaph for the former Labour leader', www.dailymail.co.uk/news/article-8190333/Boris-Johnsons-colourful-collection-insults.html (accessed 10/07/2023).

111. Ibid.
112. Ibid.
113. Ibid.
114. Ibid.
115. Ibid.
116. Ibid.
117. Ibid.
118. Ibid.
119. Ibid.

p. 133: ANSWERS: BRITANNIA UNHINGED
120. Alex Spence, 'Some Of Boris Johnson's Top Ministers Wrote A Book Calling Young Britons Lazy And Idle', www. buzzfeed.com/alexspence/britannia-unchained-boris-johnson-ministers-book (accessed 10/07/2023).

121. Ibid.
122. Ibid.
123. Ibid.
124. Ibid.

NOTES